T.V. MANIA!

Okay, tube-watchers, so you think you know your stuff? It's time to show off your network knowledge and channel your T.V. hours into trivia gold!

First prime yourself with these prime-time ticklers:

— In *Bewitched:* What did Samantha do to invoke her witchly powers?
— In *Get Smart:* By what name was Thaddeus better known?
— In *I Dream of Jeannie:* Were Tony Nelson and Jeannie married?
— In *Gilligan's Island:* What was the name of the movie star?
— In *All in the Family:* What was the name of Gloria's child?
— In *McHale's Navy:* What was "Old Lead Bottom's" name?
— In *Mary Hartman, Mary Hartman:* Who was the Fernwood Flasher?
— In *Star Trek:* Who did Majel Barrett play?
— In *It Takes a Thief:* Who played Al Mundy's father?
— In *I Love Lucy:* What was Lucy Ricardo's maiden name?

For the answers to these and a thousand others, keep on reading. Surrender yourself to a hit series of tantalizing T.V. teasers and become the prime-time prima donna of TRIVIA MANIA!

TELEVISION

TRIVIA
Mania

XAVIER EINSTEIN

ZEBRA BOOKS
KENSINGTON PUBLISHING CORP.

For Sharra and Gary, two beautiful children whose patience and understanding endured throughout this project.

ZEBRA BOOKS

are published by

Kensington Publishing Corp.
475 Park Avenue South
New York, N.Y. 10016

Fourth printing:November 1984

Printed in the United States of America

TRIVIA MANIA: *Television*

1) Who produced the series *The Untouchables?*

2) What was the name of the series in which the characters Judge Henry Garth and Trampas appeared?

3) What was the name of the Seaview's sister ship in the adventure series *Voyage to the Bottom of the Sea?*

4) Who played the part of Lt. Richard "Rip" Riddle in the adventure series *The Wackiest Ship in the Army?*

5) What was the most noted feature of Davy Crockett's appearance when seen on *Walt Disney?*

6) In one of the segments of the musical variety show *The Sonny and Cher Comedy Hour*, Cher portrayed this housewife character.

7) What character did Majel Barrett portray in the science fiction space show *Star Trek?*

8) What type of car did Starsky use in the police series *Starsky and Hutch?*

9) Who played the part of Richard Diamond in the detective series *Richard Diamond, Private Detective?*

. . . *Answers*

1. Quinn Martin

2. *The Virginian*

3. *Polidor*

4. Gary Collins

5. His coonskin cap

6. Laverne

7. Nurse Christine Chapel

8. 1974 Ford Torino

9. David Janssen

QUESTIONS

10) Name the town and state in which Micah Torrance was the marshall in the western *The Rifleman*.

11) Burt Reynolds played the part of Ben Frazer in which adventure series?

12) Name the actor who portrayed Bulldog Lovey in the series *Adventures in Paradise*.
   a. Henry Slate
   b. James Holden
   c. George Tobias
   d. Guy Stockwell

13) Name the Mexican sidekick of Kit Carson in the series *The Adventures of Kit Carson*.
   a. Amigo
   b. Tonto
   c. Taco
   d. El Toro

14) What was the name of the city defended by the "Dynamic Duo" of the *Batman* fantasy adventure?

15) What was the name of the hospital in the medical drama *Ben Casey?*

16) What was the name of the hillbilly family who struck it rich in oil in the sitcom *The Beverly Hillbillies?*

17) In the sitcom *Harper Valley P.T.A.* what actress portrayed Stella Johnson?

18) In the western *Have Gun Will Travel* who portrayed Paladin?

. . . Answers

10. North Fork, New Mexico

11. *Riverboat*

12. a. Henry Slate

13. d. El Toro

14. Gotham City

15. County General Hospital

16. Clampett

17. Barbara Eden

18. Richard Boone

19) On which network or networks was the western *Have Gun Will Travel* shown?
   a. CBS
   b. NBC
   c. ABC
   d. NBC and CBS

20) What was the name of the building which housed the Americans in the sitcom *Hogan's Heroes?*

21) What actress portrayed Honey West in the detective series *Honey West?*

22) Who was *not* a waitress in the sitcom *It's a Living?*
   a. Lois
   b. Dot
   c. Jody
   d. Vicki

23) What actress portrayed Janis Stewart in the sitcom *It's Always Jan?*

24) Jack Benny of *The Jack Benny Show* was supposedly 42 years old. True or False?

25) What was the name of Cisco Kid's horse in the western *The Cisco Kid?*

26) Who was Cheyenne Bodie's sidekick in the western *Cheyenne?*

27) Who portrayed Sam Colt, Jr. in the western series *Colt .45?*

28) Name the actor who portrayed Sgt. Chip Saunders in the series *Combat.*

. . . Answers

19. a. CBS

20. Stalag 13

21. Anne Francis

22. c. Jody

23. Janis Paige

24. False, age 39

25. Diablo

26. Smitty

27. Donald May

28. Vic Morrow

29) In the western *The Deputy* who played Marshal Simon Fry?

30) Who was the creator and also the actor who portrayed Alan Brady in the sitcom *The Dick Van Dyke Show?*

31) What were the names of the Congressman's two boys in the sitcom *The Farmer's Daughter?*

32) What was the name of the youngest of the Anderson children in the sitcom *Father Knows Best?*

33) Who was the creator of the series *Fernwood 2-Night?*

34) By what name was Thaddeus better known as in the sitcom *Get Smart?*

35) In the sitcom *The Ghost and Mrs. Muir* who played Mrs. Carolyn Muir?

36) What was the name of Gidget's boyfriend in the sitcom *Gidget?*
    a. Darin
    b. Andrew
    c. Gary
    d. Jeff

37) In the adventure series *The Buccaneers*, Dan Tempest was a reformed criminal. True or False?

38) What was the name of the small robot given to Buck by Dr. Huer in the science fiction series *Buck Rogers in the 25th Century?*

39) Who was the female counterpart of Boris Badenov in the cartoon *The Bullwinkle Show?*

. . . Answers

29. Henry Fonda

30. Carl Reiner

31. Danny and Steve

32. Kathy

33. Norman Lear

34. "The Chief"

35. Hope Lange

36. d. Jeff

37. False, a reformed pirate

38. Twiki

39. Natasha Fatale

QUESTIONS

40) In the cartoon series *The Jetsons* what was the name of the Jetsons' daughter?

41) In the police series *Joe Forrester* who portrayed Joe Forrester?

42) What was the name of Joey Barnes's kid brother in the sitcom *The Joey Bishop Show?*

43) Major John Foster became the headmaster of this school for girls in the sitcom *The John Forsythe Show*.
    a. Foster School
    b. Slade School
    c. Bright School
    d. Dame School

44) What actor portrayed Murdoch Lancer in the western *Lancer?*

45) In the science fiction series *Land of the Giants*, how many people were stranded in the world of giants?
    a. four
    b. five
    c. six
    d. seven

46) What actor portrayed Jonesy in the western *Laramie?*

47) Wyatt moved to Dodge City after leaving this small Kansas town in the western *The Life and Legend of Wyatt Earp*.

48) Who served as Wyatt's deputy in Dodge City before becoming a county sheriff in the western *The Life and Legend of Wyatt Earp?*

49) Who was the leader of the "Ten Percent Gang" in the western *The Life and Legend of Wyatt Earp?*

. . . Answers

40. Judy

41. Lloyd Bridges

42. Larry

43. a. Foster School

44. Andrew Duggan

45. d. seven

46. Hoagy Carmichael

47. Ellsworth

48. Bat Masterson

49. Old Man Clanton

50) Who was the principal in the drama series *Lucas Tanner?*

51) What was the theme song of the sitcom M*A*S*H?

52) What was Hawkeye's full name in the sitcom M*A*S*H?

53) The goal in this quiz show was to determine the real identity of the costumed celebrity-contestants.

54) Who was Maude's divorced daughter in the sitcom *Maude?*

55) Who were the three sons of ranching baron Ben Cartwright in the western *Bonanza?*

56) Who was McCloud's superior in the police series *McCloud?*

57) Who did Jerry Buell marry in the sitcom *The Mothers-in-Law?*

58) Where did Herman Munster have a job in the sitcom *The Munsters?*
    a. funeral home
    b. lawn care company
    c. insecticide plant
    d. antique shop

59) Gillmore Cobb of the sitcom *My Favorite Husband* was a shipping magnate. True or False?

60) What subject did Miss Brooks teach in the sitcom *Our Miss Brooks?*
    a. Geography
    b. History
    c. Mathematics
    d. English

. . . *Answers*

50. Margaret Blumenthal

51. "Suicide is Painless"

52. Capt. Benjamin Franklin Pierce

53. *Masquerade Party*

54. Carol

55. Hoss, Adam, and Little Joe

56. Chief Peter B. Clifford

57. Susie Hubbard

58. a. funeral home

59. False, peanut magnate

60. d. English

61) What was Danny Williams's profession in the sitcom *Make Room for Daddy?*
    a. television producer
    b. sports announcer
    c. radio personality
    d. nightclub entertainer

62) What was the name and breed of the Williams' dog in the sitcom *Make Room for Daddy?*

63) What sport would identify Guido Panzini of the *Jack Paar Show?*
    a. bowling
    b. tennis
    c. golf
    d. baseball

64) Who was the adopted son of the Douglas family in the sitcom *My Three Sons?*

65) What actor portrayed John Monroe in the sitcom *My World and Welcome to It?*

66) Who were the Blues Brothers on NBC's *Saturday Night Live?*

67) What actor portrayed Glenn Howard in the adventure series *The Name of the Game?*

68) Steve McQueen played Josh Randall, a bounty hunter in this western series aired from 1958 to 1961.

69) What was the name of the high school at which Gabe Kotter taught in the series *Welcome Back, Kotter?*

70) What was the character name of the marshal played by Joel McCrea on *Wichita Town?*

. . . Answers

61. d. nightclub entertainer

62. Laddie, terrier

63. c. golf

64. Ernie

65. William Windom

66. Dan Aykroyd and John Belushi

67. Gene Barry

68. *Wanted: Dead or Alive*

69. James Buchanan High

70. Mike Dunbar

QUESTIONS

71) Who played the part of Cameron Garrett Brooks in the sitcom *Window on Main Street?*

72) What was the name of the island from which Wonder Woman was discovered by Major Steve Trevor in the series *Wonder Woman?*

73) What adventure series featured actor Dean Fredericks in the leading role and employed the use of Air Force bases in many of its sets?

74) What breed of dogs were given as gifts on the talk show *The Stork Club?*

75) What actor played the part of Inspector Dan Robbins in *The Streets of San Francisco?*

76) What was the name of the highly controversial quiz show aired during the 1950s which was emceed by Warren Hull?

77) The plays shown on *Studio One* were live performances. True or False?

78) Where was the home and office for the detectives on *Surfside Six?*

79) Tom Selleck portrayed which character in the detective series *The Rockford Files?*
   a. Lt. Chapman
   b. Lance White
   c. John Cooper
   d. Joseph "Rocky" Rockford

80) What was the name of the teacher played by Lloyd Haynes in the series *Room 222?*

. . . Answers

71. Robert Young

72. Paradise Island

73. Steve Canyon

74. Welsh Terriers or Boxers

75. Richard Hatch

76. *Strike It Rich*

77. True

78. A houseboat

79. b. Lance White

80. Pete Dixon

QUESTIONS

81) Name the actor who played the part of Chicken George in *Roots*.

82) The part of John Reynolds was played by which actor in the drama *Roots?*
    a. Vic Morrow
    b. Lloyd Bridges
    c. Burl Ives
    d. Lorne Greene

83) What was the name of the actor who played the part of Tod Stiles in the series *Route 66?*

84) Name the officer that Gary Crosby played in the police drama *Adam 12*.

85) Jackie Coogan portrayed this character in *The Addams Family* sitcom.

86) What was the middle name of Morticia Addams in *The Addams Family?*
    a. Pugsley
    b. Thursday
    c. Frump
    d. Cousin

87) In the sitcom *Amos 'N' Andy*, George Stevens held a position of authority amongst his lodge brothers in which he took this name.

88) Who did Patrick Macnee portray in the spy drama *The Avengers?*

89) Who did Noreen Corcoran play in *Bachelor Father?*

90) Who replaced Kitty Russel as operator of the Long-branch Saloon in the western *Gunsmoke?*

. . . Answers

81. Ben Vereen

82. d. Lorne Greene

83. Martin Milner

84. Officer Ed Wells

85. Uncle Fester

86. c. Frump

87. "Kingfish"

88. Jonathan Steed

89. Kelly Gregg, Bentley's niece

90. Miss Hannah

91) How many years did the western series *Gunsmoke* run?
    a. 10 years
    b. 15 years
    c. 20 years
    d. 25 years

92) What was the name of Hank's baby sister in the sitcom *Hank?*

93) In *The Hardy Boys Mysteries* what actor portrayed Joe Hardy?

94) How many prospective brides left Massachusetts for the frontier in the comedy series *Here Come the Brides?*
    a. 25
    b. 50
    c. 75
    d. 100

95) What type of empire did Big John Cannon wish to establish in the western *The High Chaparral?*
    a. race horse
    b. cattle
    c. fur
    d. tobacco

96) What character did Bill Bixby portray in the adventure series *The Incredible Hulk?*

97) In the western *The Iron Horse* what did Ben Calhoun win in a poker game?
    a. hotel
    b. railroad
    c. wagontrain
    d. horse

. . . *Answers*

91. c. 20 years

92. Tina

93. Shaun Cassidy

94. d. 100

95. b. cattle

96. David Bruce Banner

97. b. railroad

98) Who played Al Mundy's father in the intrigue series *It Takes a Thief?*

99) Which actress portrays Nancy Beebe in the sitcom *It's a Living?*

100) Who was the voice of Charlie Townsend in the detective series *Charlie's Angels?*

101) What actor portrayed Don Corey in the detective drama *Checkmate?*

102) What was the name of Raul's aunt in the sitcom *Chico and the Man?*

103) What was the name of the sheriff in the western *Cimarron City?*

104) *The Danny Thomas Show* featured Danny Thomas in the role of Danny White. True or False?

105) Who was the sponsor of the western *Death Valley Days?*

106) On what major network did the sitcom *December Bride* appear?

107) *The Defenders* became a series after a telecast entitled *The Defender* which starred which two actors as the father and son lawyers?

108) Who portrayed Dusty in the sitcom *Dusty's Trail?*

109) What was the name of the first Bradford grandchild in the series *Eight is Enough?*
    a. Sarah Ann
    b. Jamie Lynne
    c. Beth Ann
    d. Sandra Sue

. . . Answers

98. Fred Astaire

99. Marian Mercer

100. John Forsythe

101. Anthony George

102. Aunt Charo

103. Lane Temple

104. False, Danny Williams

105. 20 Mule Team borax

106. CBS

107. Ralph Bellamy and William Shatner

108. Bob Denver

109. d. Sandra Sue

110) In the sitcom *Ensign O'Toole*, Jay C. Flippen portrayed Ensign O'Toole. True or False?

111) In the sitcom *F Troop* what actor portrayed Capt. Wilton Parmenter?

112) On what island did the war drama *From Here to Eternity* take place?

113) Dr. Richard Kimble was accused of killing his mother in the series *The Fugitive*. True or False?

114) Which actress portrayed Susanna Pomeroy in the sitcom *The Gale Storm Show?*

115) In the sitcom *The George Burns and Gracie Allen Show* what was the name of Gracie's cohort and neighbor?

116) What was the name of Mr. Henley's girlfriend in the adventure series *The Greatest American Hero?*

117) What was the name of the handyman who helped in the restoration of the Douglas' farm in the sitcom *Green Acres?*

118) What actor portrayed Marshal Matt Dillon in the western *Gunsmoke?*

119) What was the name of the doctor in the western *Gunsmoke?*

120) In *The Jackie Gleason Show: The American Scene Magazine* who traveled the country in search of new talent to be exposed on the show?

121) In the medical series *Janet Dean, Registered Nurse*, who portrayed Janet Dean?

. . . Answers

110. False, Dean Jones portrayed Ensign O'Toole

111. Ken Berry

112. Hawaii

113. False, accused of killing his wife

114. Gale Storm

115. Blanche Morton

116. Pam Davidson

117. Eb Dawson

118. James Arness

119. Dr. Galen (Doc) Adams

120. George Jessel

121. Ella Raines

122) Which of the following characterizations was *not* portrayed in *The Jerry Lewis Show?*
    a. The Nutty Professor
    b. The Poor Soul
    c. Ralph Rotten
    d. Clever Clyde

123) Theo Kojak and Frank McNeil were at one time partners in the police series *Kojak.* True or False?

124) Who played the part of Keeglefarven in *The Red Buttons Show?*

125) Mercer General was the name of the hospital in the drama *Dr. Kildare.* True or False?

126) What was the name of the bearded companion of Flash Gordon in the science fiction series *Flash Gordon?*

127) What character did Frank Sutton portray in the sitcom *Gomer Pyle, U.S.M.C.?*

128) What was the name of the ranch in the western *Bonanza?*

129) In what year did the Lennon Sisters leave *The Lawrence Welk Show?*
    a. 1964
    b. 1966
    c. 1968
    d. 1970

130) What was the name of the chimp in the adventure series *Tarzan?*

131) What actor portrayed Neil Brock in the drama series *East Side/West Side?*

. . . Answers

122. d. Clever Clyde

123. True

124. Red Buttons

125. False, Blair General

126. Dr. Zharkov

127. Sgt. Vince Carter

128. Ponderosa Ranch

129. c. 1968

130. Cheetah

131. George C. Scott

132) What vehicle was used for transportation in the sitcom *The Partridge Family?*
    a. van
    b. car
    c. tractor trailer
    d. bus

133) Which actress portrayed Mary Hartman in the soap *Mary Hartman, Mary Hartman?*

134) Who played the part of the little old lady on the park bench in the series *Rowan & Martin's Laugh-In?*

135) Whose voice provided the sounds for Jack's Maxwell in The *Jack Benny Show?*

136) What character did Donna Douglas portray in the sitcom *The Beverly Hillbillies?*

137) When Eve Arden first starred in the sitcom *Our Miss Brooks*, she was making $4000 per week. True or False?

138) What was the name of Bullwinkle's squirrel friend in the cartoon *The Bullwinkle Show?*

139) What was the name of the ranch on *The Roy Rogers Show?*

140) Socrates "Sock" Miller is a Bureau of Fish and Wildlife Ornithologist who is studying to become a forest ranger in the sitcom *The People's Choice*. True or False?

141) What part was played by Henry Calvin in the western *Zorro?*

142) Who was Jack Benny's valet in *The Jack Benny Show?*

. . . Answers

132. d. bus

133. Louise Lasser

134. Ruth Buzzi

135. Mel Blanc

136. Elly May Clampett

137. True

138. Rocket J. Squirrel or Rocky

139. Double R Bar Ranch

140. False, he was studying to become a lawyer

141. Sgt. Garcia

142. Eddie "Rochester" Anderson

143) How did Samantha Stephens of the sitcom *Bewitched* invoke her witchly powers?
    a. meditated
    b. waved her hands
    c. nodded her head
    d. twitched her nose

144) Which actress portrayed Kaye Buell in the sitcom *The Mothers-in-Law?*

145) In the sitcom *All in the Family*, what was the name of Gloria's child?

146) Who was Larry's engineer in the sitcom *Hello, Larry?*

147) Who was Patty Lane's younger brother in the sitcom *The Patty Duke Show?*

148) What was the cover used by Kelly Robinson in the adventure series *I Spy?*
    a. tennis player
    b. football player
    c. bowler
    d. chess champion

149) Who was the older brother in the sitcom *The Brothers?*

150) During the 1962 and 1963 Christmas season a cartoon version of Dickens' *The Christmas Carol* featured this cartoon character as Ebeneezer Scrooge.

151) Who was the notorious doctor in the science fiction series *Lost in Space?*

152) Who portrayed Buck Webb in the sitcom *The Doris Day Show?*

. . . Answers

143. d. twitched her nose

144. Kaye Ballard

145. Joey

146. Earl

147. Ross Lane

148. a. tennis player

149. Harvey Box

150. Mr. Magoo

151. Dr. Zachary Smith

152. Denver Pyle

153) Natalie Wood portrayed this character in the war drama *From Here to Eternity.*

154) Included in each episode of the cartoon *The Alvin Show* was an inventor by this name.

155) What character did Danny Thomas portray in the sitcom *I'm a Big Girl Now?*

156) What was the first soap opera to become a major hit in prime time?

157) In the sitcom *The Good Life* Albert and Jane Miller cast aside their middle class jobs to become a butler and cook. True or False?

158) In what T.V. western series was Clint Eastwood featured?

159) In the western *Broken Arrow*, what was the name of the Apache Chief portrayed by Michael Ansara?

160) Who portrayed Oscar North in the sitcom *He and She?*

161) How many kids did Mike & Carol Brady have in the sitcom *The Brady Bunch?*
    a. four
    b. five
    c. six
    d. eight

162) What was the nickname of the character played by Edd Byrnes in the series *77 Sunset Strip?*

163) What was the theme song in the adventure series *The Greatest American Hero?*

. . . *Answers*

153. Karen Holmes

154. Clyde Crashcup

155. Dr. Benjamin Douglass

156. *Peyton Place*

157. True

158. *Rawhide*

159. Cochise

160. Jack Cassidy

161. c. six

162. "Kookie"

163. "Believe It or Not"

164) What was the name of the syndicated documentary series hosted by John Kieran?

165) What was the name of the saloon opened by Lily Merrill in the western *The Lawman?*

166) What type of dog was Rin Tin Tin in *The Adventures of Rin Tin Tin?*

167) Carson City was the name of the city in the western *Gunsmoke.* True or False?

168) What character was played by James Darren in the series *The Time Tunnel?*

169) What does Elly May of *The Beverly Hillbillies* call her pets?

170) What was the name of Tonto's horse in the western *The Lone Ranger?*

171) Who portrayed Tom Lopaka in the detective series *Hawaiian Eye?*

172) What actor portrayed Dobie Gillis in the sitcom *The Many Loves of Dobie Gillis?*

173) Where were the Baxters transferred in the sitcom *Hazel?*
   a. Africa
   b. Japan
   c. Greece
   d. Middle East

174) In the sitcom *All in the Family*, what was the name of Edith's cousin who eventually got her own show?

. . . *Answers*

164. *Kieran's Kaleidoscope*

165. Birdcage Saloon

166. German Shepherd

167. False, Dodge City

168. Dr. Tony Newman

169. critters

170. Scout

171. Bob Conrad

172. Dwayne Hickman

173. d. Middle East

174. Maude

QUESTIONS

175) What was the name of Velvet Brown's horse in the adventure series *National Velvet?*
    a. Star
    b. Jumper
    c. King
    d. Dusty

176) What high school was Stu Erwin principal of in the sitcom *The Stu Erwin Show?*

177) In the western *Daniel Boone*, what actor played Daniel Boone?

178) What was the name of Eddie's father in the series *The Courtship of Eddie's Father?*

179) What was the name of the sketch in which characters Willard and his wife Margaret were featured in *The Jonathan Winters Show?*

180) "This tape will self-destruct in five seconds" was part of a taped message presented to a government agent at the beginning of each episode in this intrigue series.

181) What gangster was Eliot Ness's arch enemy in the series *The Untouchables?*

182) Who was the seven foot tall character who resembled Frankenstein in the sitcom *The Munsters?*

183) In the series *Wonder Woman*, what was the name of the actor who played Major Steve Trevor?

184) Who joined Jane Curtin as a newscaster when an anchor team was created on NBC's *Saturday Night Live?*

. . . Answers

175. c. King

176. Hamilton High School

177. Fess Parker

178. Tom Corbett

179. "Couple Up the Street"

180. *Mission: Impossible*

181. Al Capone

182. Herman Munster

183. Lyle Waggoner

184. Dan Aykroyd

185) William King Driggs was the youngest member of the King family in the musical variety show *The King Family Show*. True or False?

186) In *The Adventures of Wild Bill Hickok*, what was the name of Wild Bill's horse?
    a. Joker
    b. Buckshot
    c. Fireball
    d. Surefoot

187) In the comedy series *Here Come the Brides* who portrayed Jeremy Bolt?

188) What was Sgt. Suzanne Anderson's nickname in the police series *Police Woman?*

189) Caine was taught by these two masters as a youth in China in the series *Kung Fu*.

190) Which actress portrayed Stephanie Mills, a niece adopted by the Bunkers in the sitcom *All in the Family?*

191) Who was the female member of the Impossible Missions Force in the intrigue series *Mission: Impossible?*

192) What was the title of the soap opera in *The Carol Burnett Show?*

193) The characters of the sitcom M*A*S*H were members of this Mobile Army Surgical Hospital?
    a. 1077th
    b. 1177th
    c. 3077th
    d. 4077th

194) What was the name of the quiz show of the 1950's in which the winners were always given silver dollars?

. . . Answers

185. False, he was the oldest

186. b. Buckshot

187. Bobby Sherman

188. Pepper

189. Master Po and Master Kan

190. Danielle Brisebois

191. Cinnamon Carter

192. "As the Stomach Turns"

193. d. 4077th

194. *Doctor I.Q.*

195) What was the name of the song which made the Partridge family a success in the sitcom *The Partridge Family?*

196) Ann Marie and Don Hollinger were married before the sitcom *That Girl* was taken off the air. True or False?

197) Which actress portrayed Irma Peterson in the sitcom *My Friend Irma?*

198) What was the single and most unique feature associated with Cosmo Topper in the sitcom *Topper?*

199) In the sitcom *The Brian Keith Show*, what character did Brian Keith portray?

200) What were the names of Jason Bolt's two younger brothers in the comedy series *Here Come the Brides?*

201) What actor played Inspector Steve Keller on *The Streets of San Francisco?*

202) The character of Jonathan Garvey was portrayed by this former Los Angeles Rams football star in the series *Little House on the Prairie.*

203) Who was the narrator of the documentary series *The 20th Century?*

204) Who was Clinton Judd's young assistant in the series *Judd, for the Defense?*

205) Who was the soap opera star of the soap in which Dick Preston landed a job in the sitcom *The New Dick Van Dyke Show?*

206) John Belushi played the part of Gary Ewing in the series *Dallas.* True or False?

. . . *Answers*

195. "I Think I Love You"

196. False

197. Marie Wilson

198. He was the only one who could hear and see the ghosts

199. Dr. Sean Jamison

200. Jeremy and Joshua

201. Michael Douglas

202. Merlin Olsen

203. Walter Cronkite

204. Ben Caldwell

205. Margot Brighton

206. False, David Ackroyd and later Ted Shackelford

207) Who was Marcus Welby's assistant in the medical series *Marcus Welby, M.D.?*

208) Who managed the U.N.C.L.E. headquarters in the spy series *The Man from U.N.C.L.E.?*

209) When Madison High was demolished for a highway project in the sitcom *Our Miss Brooks,* Miss Brooks found a job at another high school. True or False?

210) Name the series whose reporters worked for the Trans-Globe Wire Service.

211) What was the name of Fish's wife in the sitcom *Fish?*

212) What actor portrayed Dr. Joe Gannon in the medical series *Medical Center?*

213) What actor portrayed Zeb Macahan in the western *How the West was Won?*

214) In the sitcom *Life with Elizabeth* which actress portrayed Elizabeth?

215) What was the name of the ranch on which Sky King lived in the series *Sky King?*

216) Barbara Cason portrayed this policewoman in the sitcom *Carter Country.*

217) What agent was paired with April Dancer in the spy series *The Girl from U.N.C.L.E.?*

218) Who was the first owner-companion of Lassie in the adventure series *Lassie?*

219) Who played Joe Gerard in the series *Rhoda?*

. . . *Answers*

207. Dr. Steven Kiley

208. Mr. Alexander Waverly

209. False, Mrs. Nestor's Private Elementary School

210. *Wire Service*

211. Bernice

212. Chad Everett

213. James Arness

214. Betty White

215. Flying Crown Ranch

216. Cloris Phebus

217. Mark Slade

218. Jeff Miller

219. David Groh

QUESTIONS

220) Who was the older Darrell brother in the series *The Lawyers?*

221) What actor portrayed Det. Chin Ho Kelly in the police series *Hawaii Five-O?*

222) In the fantasy adventure *Batman*, Burgess Meredith portrayed which character?
   a. The Riddler
   b. The Joker
   c. The Penguin
   d. Egghead

223) What was the name of the TV news producer that Mary Richards worked for in the sitcom *The Mary Tyler Moore Show?*

224) What character did actor Robert Urich portray in the police drama *S.W.A.T.?*

225) This actress, who became Felix's girlfriend in the sitcom *The Odd Couple*, portrayed Jim Anderson's oldest daughter in *Father Knows Best.*

226) What was the original title for the show *You Asked for It?*

227) Whose orchestra performed on *The Jackie Gleason Show* in the 1950s?

228) This actor replaced Henry Silva as the character Kane in the science fiction series *Buck Rogers in the 25th Century.*

229) In the crime series *The Green Hornet* what was the "civilized" name of the Green Hornet?

230) What character did Frances Bavier play in the sitcom *The Andy Griffith Show?*

. . . *Answers*

220. Brian

221. Kam Fong

222. c. The Penguin

223. Lou Grant

224. Officer Jim Street

225. Elinor Donahue

226. *The Art Baker Show*

227. Ray Bloch's

228. Michael Ansara

229. Britt Reid

230. Aunt Bee Taylor

231) *Mork & Mindy* was a spinoff from a *Happy Days* episode which featured the attempted kidnap of Richie Cunningham by an alien from the planet Ork. True or False?

232) What was the first name of George MacMichael's sister in the sitcom *The Real McCoys?*

233) What is the name of the cruise ship in the sitcom *The Love Boat?*

234) In the sitcom *F Troop* what was the name of the cowgirl intent on marrying Capt. Parmenter?

235) In the adventure series *The Bionic Woman*, what is the other name of the Bionic Woman?

236) The sitcom *The Donna Reed Show* was set in this town.
   a. Hilldale
   b. Woodstown
   c. Birchrunville
   d. Rolling Hills

237) What character did Virginia Stefan portray in the intrigue series *I Led Three Lives?*

238) This quiz show, emceed by Art Linkletter, ran from September 1954 to April 1961 and involved contestants performing stunts.

239) Frank McNeil became chief of detectives for this precinct in the series *Kojak*.
   a. 5th
   b. 12th
   c. 13th
   d. 15th

240) What type of car was used in the series *Route 66?*

. . . *Answers* .

231. True

232. Flora

233. *Pacific Princess*

234. Wrangler Jane

235. Jaime Sommers

236. a. Hilldale

237. Eva Philbrick

238. *People Are Funny*

239. c. 13th

240. Corvette

41) David Niven was a regular in the drama *Four Star Playhouse*. True or False?

42) What was the name of the apartments which housed the Jetsons in the cartoon series *The Jetsons?*

43) In the detective series Boston Blackie, what was the Inspector's name?

44) Who did Thelma Evans marry in the sitcom *Good Times?*

45) In the adventure series *Gentle Ben* what was the name of Ben's young companion?

46) This producer of *Adam 12* was best known for his work in the hit series *Dragnet.*

47) What actress first portrayed Nancy Drew in the adventure series *The Hardy Boys Mysteries?*

48) What agency did John Drake work for in the series *Secret Agent?*

49) This actress, who portrayed Maude's first maid in the sitcom *Maude*, left the show two years later to star in her own program *Good Times*.

50) What was the name of "The Man's" garage in the sitcom *Chico and the Man?*

51) Billy Blue's mother was killed by a gunshot wound in the western *The High Chaparral*. True or False?

52) In the sitcom *The Danny Thomas Show*, what actor portrayed Rosey Robbins?

. . . Answers

241. True

242. Skypad Apartments

243. Inspector Faraday

244. Keith Anderson

245. Mark Wedloe

246. Jack Webb

247. Pamela Sue Martin

248. The British Government

249. Esther Rolle

250. Ed's Garage

251. False, an Apache arrow

252. Roosevelt Grier

253) What was the name of the boat in the adventures series *Riverboat?*

254) Agent 99 was played by Barbara Feldon, in the sitcom *Get Smart. What was her real name?*

255) What actor portrayed Robert Ironside in the police series *Ironside?*

256) In the drama series *Executive Suite* what character did Mitchell Ryan portray?

257) What was the name of the outlaw brothers in the western *The Life and Legend of Wyatt Earp?*

258) What was the name of the city in the western *The Deputy?*

    a. Virginia City
    b. Dodge City
    c. Silver City
    d. Oklahoma City

259) What was the name of Prof. James K. Howard's son in the sitcom *The Jimmy Stewart Show?*

260) What actor portrayed Det. Sgt. Sam Stone in the police drama *Felony Squad?*

261) Name the actor who played Jim Bowie in *The Adventures of Jim Bowie.*

262) What were the names of the prehistoric couple introduced to the 20th century by the astronauts in the sitcom *It's About Time?*

. . . Answers

253. *Enterprise*

254. Susan Hilton

255. Raymond Burr

256. Don Walling

257. Thompson brothers

258. c. Silver City

259. Peter

260. Howard Duff

261. Scott Forbes

262. Shad and Gronk

263) What weapon was most frequently used by Cisco's pal Poncho in the western *The Cisco Kid?*
    a. hand gun
    b. rifle
    c. knife
    d. bullwhip

264) Which character is known for the monocle he wore in the sitcom *Hogan's Heroes?*

265) James Doohan played "Scotty" in the series *Star Trek*, in what capacity did he serve?

266) In the sitcom *The Lucy Show* what character did Lucille Ball portray?

267) What actor portrayed Dr. Michael Upton in the sitcom *Doctor in the House?*

268) What was the name of the multibillionaire in the series *The Millionaire?*

269) What was the name of the villainess who re-programmed Tobor to the evil ways in the childrens' series *Captain Video and His Video Rangers?*

270) What series is associated with the characters Frank Nitti, Martin Flaherty, William Youngfellow and Enrico Rossi?

271) In this series a voice would announce: "There is nothing wrong with your TV set. We are controlling transmission."

272) In the sitcom *The Donna Reed Show* what character did Donna Reed portray?

273) Who were the two families featured in the sitcom *The Mothers-in-Law?*

. . . *Answers*

263. d. bullwhip

264. Col. Klink

265. Engineer

266. Lucy Carmichael

267. Barry Evans

268. John Beresford Tipton

269. Atar

270. *The Untouchables*

271. *The Outer Limits*

272. Donna Stone

273. Hubbards and Buells

274) What actor portrayed Lt. Mike Parker in the police series *Naked City?*

275) Clark Kent of *The Adventures of Superman* was born under this name on a faraway planet.

276) Cowgirl Laurie Anders was a regular in this variety series of the early 1950s.

277) The prisoner of the adventure series *The Prisoner* was known by this number.

278) What character did Robert Karnes portray in the police series *The Lawless Years?*

279) What was Paul Morgan's profession on the series *The Tab Hunter Show?*

280) What was the name of Caine's American cousin who appeared in the final season of the series *Kung Fu?*

281) What character did Bill Bixby portray in the sitcom *My Favorite Martian?*

282) In the police series *Hawaii Five-O*, the Five-O group were members of the Honolulu Police Department. True or False?

283) What brand of cigarettes did Sgt. Bilko smoke on the sitcom *The Phil Silvers Show?*

284) What actor portrayed Tom Jeffords in the western *Broken Arrow?*

285) What was the name of the superintendent of the Hollister's apartment building in the sitcom *He & She?*

. . . *Answers*

274. Horace McMahon

275. Kal-El

276. *The Ken Murray Show*

277. Number 6

278. Max

279. Cartoonist

280. Margit McLean

281. Tim O'Hara

282. False

283. Camel

284. John Lupton

285. Andrew Hummel

286) What was the table number at which the celebrities sat when being interviewed on *The Stork Club?*

287) In what city was the police series *The Lineup* set?
a. San Diego
b. San Jose
c. San Francisco
d. Los Angeles

288) Which department of the U.S. Government employed Eliot Ness in the series *The Untouchables?*

289) What was the name of Julia's young son in the sitcom *Julia?*

290) What actor portrayed Richard Richardson in the sitcom *The New Dick Van Dyke Show?*

291) Who played Tom Corbett in the series *The Courtship of Eddie's Father?*

292) Who was the female character of the sitcom *The Many Loves of Dobie Gillis* who was intent on marrying Dobie?

293) The adventure series *Waterfront* featured John Herrick as a captain of this tugboat.

294) How many children did Mama and Papa Hansen have in the comedy series *Mama?*

295) This sheriff, who was the lead character in another sitcom, confronted Danny Williams in an episode of *Make Room for Daddy* for running a stop sign in this Southern community.

296) In the cartoon series *The Flintstones* a baby elephant with a long trunk was used as the Flintstones vacuum cleaner. True or False?

. . . Answers

286. 50

287. c. San Francisco

288. The Treasury Dept.

289. Corey

290. Richard Dawson

291. Bill Bixby

292. Zelda Gilroy

293. *Cheryl Ann*

294. 3

295. Andy Taylor, *The Andy Griffith Show*

296. True

297) What was "Old Lead Bottom's" name in the sitcom *McHale's Navy?*

298) What did Ralph Kramden drive in the sitcom *The Honeymooners?*
    a. cab
    b. bus
    c. train
    d. limousine

299) Where did the famous gunfight occur in the western *The Life and Legend of Wyatt Earp?*

300) What was the longest running western in the history of TV?
    a. *Bonanza*
    b. *The Big Valley*
    c. *Gunsmoke*
    d. *The Rifleman*

301) What was the name of the millionaire in the sitcom *Gilligan's Island?*

302) Daisy Cooper was a housekeeper in the western *Laramie*. True or False?

303) What was the character's name portrayed by Nick Nolte in the drama *Rich Man, Poor Man?*

304) What piece of jewelry was always seen on June Cleaver in the sitcom *Leave It to Beaver?*

305) James MacArthur portrayed this character in the police series *Hawaii Five-O*.

306) In the medical drama *Ben Casey*, Dr. Ben Casey was played by Sam Jaffe. True or False?

. . . *Answers*

297. Capt. Wallace B. Binghamton

298. b. bus

299. O.K. Corral

300. c. *Gunsmoke*

301. Thurston Howell III

302. True

303. Tom Jordache

304. pearl necklace

305. Det. Danny Williams

306. False, Vince Edwards

307) Who was the Fernwood Flasher in the soap *Mary Hartman, Mary Hartman?*

308) In the series *S.W.A.T.,* which actor played Sgt. David "Deacon" Kay?
   a. David Soul
   b. Paul Michael Glaser
   c. Rod Perry
   d. James Coleman

309) Who was the head nurse in the medical series *The Nurses?*

310) On what comedy series was the skit "The Hickenloopers"?

311) Who was the announcer in *The Jack Benny Show?*

312) This adventure series, filmed entirely in England, portrayed Robert Shaw as Captain Dan Tempest.

313) What actress portrayed Lisa Douglas in the sitcom *Green Acres?*

314) In the sitcom *Amos 'N' Andy* who portrayed Amos Jones?

315) In what profession was Mr. Peepers of the sitcom *Mr. Peepers?*
   a. teaching
   b. law
   c. medical
   d. acting

316) What was the character's name of the grandson to Grandpa Amos McCoy in the sitcom *The Real McCoys?*

. . . *Answers*

307. Raymond Larkin, Mary's grandfather

308. c. Rod Perry

309. Liz Thorpe

310. *Your Show of Shows*

311. Don Wilson

312. *The Buccaneers*

313. Eva Gabor

314. Alvin Childress

315. a. teaching

316. Luke McCoy

317) This drama series had an eight season run, utilizing letters from this hostess's fans as the content for the dramatized responses of the early season shows.

318) Which actor portrayed Sgt. Morgan O'Rourke in the sitcom *F Troop?*
   a. Forrest Tucker
   b. Larry Storch
   c. Frank DeKova
   d. Bob Steele

319) In the sitcom *Bewitched*, who portrayed Endora, Samantha Stephen's mother?

320) Who was the Stone's oldest child in the sitcom *The Donna Reed Show?*

321) Desiderio Alberto Arnaz IV was born to Lucille Ball on the same night that Lucy Ricardo gave birth to Little Ricky in *I Love Lucy*. True or False?

322) This quiz show, emceed by Allen Ludden, featured a 60 second "Lightning Round."

323) What character from a police series is known for his love of lollipops?

324) What character did LeVar Burton play in the drama *Roots?*

325) What actor portrayed Porter Ricks in the adventure series *Flipper?*

. . . *Answers*

317. *The Loretta Young Show*

318. a. Forrest Tucker

319. Agnes Moorehead

320. Mary

321. True

322. *Password*

323. Kojak

324. Klunta Kinte

325. Brian Kelly

326) Art Carney returned in the 1966-1967 season of *The Jackie Gleason Show* after an absence of how many years?
    a. four years
    b. six years
    c. nine years
    d. eleven years

327) Who was the original host of the quiz show *Break the Bank?*

328) In the sitcom *The Good Guys* what was the name of Rufus Butterworth's friend?

329) Pete Adam was the senior officer in the series *Adam 12.* True or False?

330) What actor portrayed Ben Travis in the drama *Frontier Circus?*

331) In the series *Sergeant Preston of the Yukon*, what was the name of the dog?

332) Who replaced Chester Goode in the western *Gunsmoke?*

333) This quiz show, hosted by Gene Rayburn, was based on the exactness of answers given by the six celebrities and two contestants.

334) Who was the leader of the prospective brides in the comedy series *Here Come the Brides?*

335) What character did Kate Jackson play in the detective series *Charlie's Angels?*

336) Who did Peter Lawford portray in the sitcom *Dear Phoebe?*

. . . Answers

326. c. 9 years

327. Bert Parks

328. Bert Gramus

329. False, Pete Malloy

330. John Derek

331. Yukon King

332. Festus Haggen

333. *Match Game P.M.*

334. Candy Pruitt

335. Sabrina Duncan

336. Bill Hastings

337) What was the name of the character Darren McGavin played in the show *Riverboat?*

338) In the police series *Get Christie Love* what actress portrayed Det. Christie Love?

339) What actor portrayed Tom Keating in the mini-series *The Innocent and the Damned?*

340) What was the name of the schoolteacher who Tom Bradford married in the series *Eight is Enough?*

341) What was the name of the .45s which Wyatt Earp used to keep peace in the western *The Life and Legend of Wyatt Earp?*

342) Who portrayed Joan Miller in the courtroom drama *The Defenders?*

343) Elroy was the name of the family dog in the cartoon series *The Jetsons*. True or False?

344) Which actor portrayed Frank Faraday in the series *Faraday and Company?*

345) What was the name of the captain in the series *Adventures in Paradise?*

346) Who was the supervisor in the sitcom *It's a Living?*

347) Who portrayed U.S. Marshal Jim Crown in the western *Cimarron Strip?*

348) What actor portrayed Col. Robert Hogan in the sitcom *Hogan's Heroes?*

349) What was the name of the starship captained by James T. Kirk in the series *Star Trek?*

. . . Answers

337. Grey Holden

338. Teresa Graves

339. Sam Elliott

340. Abby

341. "Buntline Special" pistols

342. Joan Hackett

343. False, Astro was the dog's name

344. Dan Dailey

345. Adam Troy

346. Nancy Beebe

347. Stuart Whitman

348. Bob Crane

349. *U.S.S. Enterprise*

350) In the drama series *Lucas Tanner*, David Hartman portrayed Lucas Tanner. True or False?

351) Who was the multibillionaire's secretary in the series *The Millionaire?*

352) Who was the producer and host of *Candid Camera?*

353) Who portrayed the character Professor Multiple in the series *Voyage to the Bottom of the Sea?*

354) What was the address of the Day family in the series *Life with Father?*

355) Who did Rob Reiner portray in *All in the Family?*

356) What was the name of Dr. Wayne Hudson's daughter in the drama *Dr. Hudson's Secret Journal?*

357) What did Roger Buell do for a living in the sitcom *The Mothers-in-Law?*
    a. commercial pilot
    b. baker
    c. lawyer
    d. television writer

358) Which one of the three sons was married to Katie Miller in the sitcom *My Three Sons?*

359) Who portrayed Ozzie Nelson in *The Adventures of Ozzie & Harriet?*

360) This sitcom was the only one of the three in the *90 Bristol Court* series to make it through the entire 1964–1965 season.

361) Who was the bookshop owner in the soap *Peyton Place?*

. . . *Answers*

350. True

351. Michael Anthony

352. Allen Funt

353. Vincent Price

354. West 48th Street, New York

355. Mike Stivic

356. Kathy

357. d. television writer

358. Robbie

359. Ozzie Nelson

360. *Karen*

361. Constance Mackenzie Carson

362) Marsha Spear was portrayed by actress Janet DeGore in the series *The Law and Mr. Jones*. True or False?

363) Who played the part of Karl Robinson in the series *Swiss Family Robinson?*

364) In the western *Lancer* which one of Murdoch Lancer's sons was the college graduate?

365) The Shepards replaced this family as the neighbors of the Coopers in the sitcom *My Favorite Husband*.

366) What was the name of the oldest Hardy boy in *The Hardy Boys Mysteries?*

367) What was the name of Dagwood's boss in the sitcom *Blondie?*

368) In the sitcom *Bridget Loves Bernie*, Bernie and Bridget Steinberg were the focal point of the show as a married couple. In real life, this actor and actress were later married. Name them.

369) What was the name of Steve Baxter's wife in the sitcom *Hazel?*

370) What military rank did Steve Canyon hold in the series *Steve Canyon?*

371) Det. Lt. Ben Guthrie was portrayed by this actor in the police series *The Lineup*.

372) This former Air Force sergeant helped Major John Foster with school business in the sitcom *The John Forsythe Show*.

373) What was the name of the female duo who performed with Tony Orlando in his musical variety show?

. . . *Answers*

362. True

363. Martin Milner

364. Scott Lancer

365. Cobbs

366. Frank

367. Julius Caesar Dithers

368. David Birney and Meredith Baxter

369. Barbara

370. Lt. Col.

371. Warner Anderson

372. Ed Robbins

373. Dawn

374) Which actress portrayed Velvet Brown in the adventure series *National Velvet?*

375) Shecky Greene played the part of Pvt. Braddock in the war show *Combat.* True or False?

376) Who was the millionaire who exploited his social status and monetary wealth in attempts to attract girls in the sitcom *The Many Loves of Dobie Gillis?*

377) Who was the character Mr. Wizard in the 1950s series *Watch Mr. Wizard?*

378) What actor portrayed Lt. Frank Ballinger in the police series *M Squad?*

379) What was the name of the high school where Miss Brooks taught in the sitcom *Our Miss Brooks?*

380) What character did Abe Vigoda portray in the sitcom *Fish?*

381) Which sergeant accompanied Sam McCloud during investigations in the police series *McCloud?*

382) Alice Kramden was first portrayed by this actress in the sitcom *The Honeymooners.*

383) What was the name of the bear who became Grizzly's constant companion in the adventure series *The Life and Times of Grizzly Adams?*
  a. Tender Heart
  b. Big Bear
  c. Ben
  d. none of these

384) Who played Ben Cartwright in the western *Bonanza?*

. . . Answers

374. Lori Martin

375. True

376. Chatsworth Osborne, Jr.

377. Don Herbert

378. Lee Marvin

379. Madison High

380. Det. Phil Fish

381. Sgt. Joe Broadhurst

382. Audrey Meadows

383. c. Ben

384. Lorne Greene

385) What character did Dawn Wells portray in the sitcom *Gilligan's Island?*

386) Who was the captain in the western *Laredo?*

387) What was the song Red Buttons sang in his series *The Red Buttons Show?*

388) Who became the second Champagne Lady on *The Lawrence Welk Show?*

389) Who was the most notorious criminal in the police series *Hawaii Five-O?*

390) In the *Batman* fantasy adventure, Robin was also known as "The Boy Wonder." What was Batman's other title?

391) In the detective series *The Vise*, Mark Saber was portrayed as a one-armed private detective. True or False?

392) Who played the lawyer Paul Bryan in the adventure series *Run for Your Life?*

393) In what series was "The Flying Fickle Finger of Fate Award" introduced?

394) What actress portrayed Gail Lucas in the medical series *The Nurses?*

395) Who was the original emcee for the quiz show *You Bet Your Life?*

396) Who was Jack's wife in *The Jack Benny Show?*

397) What was the name of Captain Dan Tempest's ship in the adventure series *The Buccaneers?*
　　a. *The Barracuda*　　　c. *The Tempest*
　　b. *The Sultana*　　　d. *The Black Ship*

... *Answers*

385. Mary Ann Summers

386. Capt. Edward Parmalee

387. "Ho-Ho" Song

388. Norma Zimmer

389. Wo Fat

390. "The Caped Crusader"

391. True

392. Ben Gazzara

393. *Rowan & Martin's Laugh-In*

394. Zina Bethune

395. Groucho Marx

396. Mary Livingston

397. b. *The Sultana*

398) What actress portrayed Pam Davidson in the adventure series *The Greatest American Hero?*

399) In what town of North Carolina was the sitcom *The Andy Griffith Show* set?

400) Who was Robinson Peepers's best friend in the sitcom *Mr. Peepers?*

401) Name the actor who played Luke McCoy in the sitcom *The Real McCoys.*

402) In the adventure series *Ramar of the Jungle*, Ramar was identified as a lion. True or False?

403) What actress portrayed Penny Robinson in the science fiction series *Lost in Space?*

404) What actress played Nancy Lawrence Maitland in the drama *Family?*

405) In the sitcom *Bewitched*, what was the name of Samantha Stephens's husband?

406) What character did Bob Crane play in the sitcom *The Donna Reed Show?*

407) What was Lucy Ricardo's maiden name in the sitcom *I Love Lucy?*

408) What character did Eddie Applegate portray in the sitcom *The Patty Duke Show?*

409) Who was the District Attorney in the series *Perry Mason?*

410) Who played the principal in the series *Room 222?*

. . . Answers

398. Connie Sellecca

399. Mayberry

400. Harvey Weskit

401. Richard Crenna

402. False, Ramar meant "Great White Doctor"

403. Angela Cartwright

404. Meredith Baxter-Birney

405. Darrin Stephens

406. Dr. Dave Kelsey

407. MacGillicuddy

408. Richard Harrison, Patty's boyfriend

409. Hamilton Burger

410. Michael Constantine

411) Who played the main character of Jim Rockford in the detective series *The Rockford Files?*

412) What actress portrayed Florence Jean (Flo) Castleberry in the sitcom *Flo?*

413) In the cartoon series *The Jetsons* what was the name of George Jetson's wife?

414) In the detective series *Boston Blackie*, what was the name of Blackie's girlfriend played by Lois Collier?

415) What actor portrayed Rufus Butterworth in the sitcom *The Good Guys?*

416) Who played Officer Pete Malloy in the series *Adam 12?*

417) How many actors portrayed Harry Morton in the sitcom *The George Burns and Gracie Allen Show?*
    a. two
    b. three
    c. four
    d. five

418) What was the name of Sergeant Preston's horse in the series *Sergeant Preston of the Yukon?*

419) What was the name of Sky King's niece in the series *Sky King?*

420) What actor portrayed Chester Goode in the western *Gunsmoke?*

421) What was the name of Maude's first maid in the sitcom *Maude?*

422) What was the name of the cabdriver in the sitcom *Hey Jeannie?*

... *Answers*

411. James Garner

412. Polly Holliday

413. Jane

414. Mary Wesley

415. Bob Denver

416. Martin Milner

417. c. four

418. Rex

419. Penny

420. Dennis Weaver

421. Florida Evans

422. Al Murray

423) In the detective series *Charlie's Angels*, Farrah Fawcett-Majors was replaced by this actress who portrayed her younger sister Kris.

424) The title of the series *Make Room for Daddy* originated from a household situation in the Thomas family which occurred after Danny's return from a tour. True or False?

425) What was the name of the adventure series which featured the characters Ted McKeever and Jim Buckley as sky-divers?

426) Maxwell Smart of the sitcom *Get Smart* often used this phrase when previous explanations were unacceptable.

427) How many interns were depicted in the medical series *The Interns?*
    a. two
    b. three
    c. four
    d. five

428) In the medical drama *The Eleventh Hour* who portrayed Dr. L. Richard Starke?

429) What character did Robert Vaughn portray in the series *The Lieutenant?*

430) What actor played Dennis Mitchell in the sitcom *Dennis the Menace?*

431) Who did Cosmo G. Spacely represent in the cartoon series *The Jetsons?*

432) What was the last name of Katy in the sitcom *The Farmer's Daughter?*

. . . Answers

423. Cheryl Ladd

424. True, the children were required to shift bedrooms in order to "make room for Daddy"

425. *Ripcord*

426. "Would you believe?"

427. d. five

428. Ralph Bellamy

429. Capt. Ray Rambridge

430. Jay North

431. George Jetson's boss

432. Holstrum

433) In *The Adventures of Ozzie & Harriet*, David Nelson completed school and emerged as a professional in which area?

    a. music   c. medicine

    b. law   d. engineering

434) What actress portrayed Cassie Cranston in the sitcom *It's a Living?*

435) Who was Cisco Kid's sidekick in the western *The Cisco Kid?*

436) What POW camp was portrayed in the sitcom *Hogan's Heroes?*

    a. Russian   c. German

    b. Japanese   d. Korean

437) Who were the two major alien forces which confronted Captain Kirk's forces in the series *Star Trek?*

438) What was the name of Chester Tate's wife in the sitcom *Soap?*

439) In the sitcom *The Lucy Show*, Lucy was a secretary to this banker.

440) "Near You," the theme song of this comedy variety series, was sung by the emcee.

441) What type of car did Frank Cannon drive in the detective drama *Cannon?*

    a. Cadillac   c. Continental

    b. Monte Carlo   d. Firebird

442) What was the most unique feature of the submarine *Seaview* in the series *Voyage to the Bottom of the Sea?*

443) What was the nickname given to Frank Nitti in the series *The Untouchables?*

. . . Answers

433. b. law

434. Ann Jillian

435. Pancho

436. c. German

437. Klingons and Romulans

438. Jessica Tate

439. Mr. Mooney

440. *Milton Berle Show*

441. c. Continental

442. It had a glass front from which one could view the ocean

443. "The Enforcer"

444) What was the profession of Clarence Day in the series *Life with Father?*

    a. taxi cab driver   c. banker
    b. teacher   d. hairdresser

445) Who did Liz Torres portray in the sitcom *All in the Family?*

446) What was the name of the professor in the sitcom *Doctor in the House?*

447) Which actress portrayed Eve Hubbard in the sitcom *The Mothers-in-Law?*

448) Who did Steve Douglas marry in the sitcom *My Three Sons?*

449) For a while in 1960 the title of the series *The Adventures of Ozzie & Harriet* was changed to this title.

450) What was the name of the semi-regular feature which starred Peg Lynch and Alan Bunce in *The Kate Smith Evening Hour?*

451) Which actress portrayed Allison Mackenzie in the soap *Peyton Place?*

452) Who was the plainsman in the western *Law of the Plainsman?*

453) What was the name of the character portrayed by Robert Wagner in the series *Switch?*

454) Name the actor who portrayed Tarzan in the adventure series with the same name.

455) What was the name of the drifter son of Murdoch Lancer in the western *Lancer?*

. . . Answers

444. c. banker

445. Teresa Betancourt

446. Loftus

447. Eve Arden

448. Barbara Harper

449. *The Adventures of the Nelson Family*

450. "Ethel and Albert"

451. Mia Farrow

452. Deputy U.S. Marshal Sam Buckhart

453. Pete Ryan

454. Ron Ely

455. Johnny Madrid Lancer

456) The Shepards replaced this family as the neighbors of the Coopers in the sitcom *My Favorite Husband*.

457) What was the name of Stella's daughter in the sitcom *Harper Valley P.T.A.*?
    a. Dee
    b. Lee
    c. Bee
    d. none of these

458) What was the name of the family dog in the sitcom *Blondie?*
    a. Pooch
    b. Ruff
    c. Freemont
    d. Daisy

459) Who played the part of Jackie on *The Stu Erwin Show* and later Zelda on *Dobie Gillis?*

460) In the sitcom *Bridget Loves Bernie* the Steinberg couple lived above a New York City delicatessen. True or False?

461) Who portrayed Hazel Burke in the sitcom *Hazel?*

462) What was the rank and character name of actor Karl Malden in the police series *The Streets of San Francisco?*

463) *Rhoda* was a spinoff from what other popular TV show?

464) What was the name of the Lone Ranger's horse in the western *The Lone Ranger?*
    a. Bullet
    b. Racer
    c. Silver
    d. Scout

. . . Answers

456. Cobbs

457. a. Dee

458. d. Daisy

459. Sheila James

460. True

461. Shirley Booth

462. Det. Lt. Mike Stone

463. *The Mary Tyler Moore Show*

464. c. Silver

465) In this quiz show created by Jack Barry, five children were asked to comment or solve problems sent in by viewers.

466) What actor portrayed the character Eliot Ness in the series *The Untouchables?*

467) Who played Sheriff Clay Hollister in the western *Tombstone Territory?*

468) Which doctor in the medical series *Noah's Ark* was confined to a wheelchair?

469) What was the name of Daniel Boone's Indian friend in the show *Daniel Boone?*

470) What actor portrayed Dr. Marcus Welby in the medical series *Marcus Welby, M.D.?*

471) What was the name of the ranch on the western *Witchita Town?*

472) In the series *Wonder Woman,* what was the substance in the gold belts and bracelets which gave her super powers?
    a. Feminum   c. Dynotron
    b. Superglow   d. Shieldanyte

473) What character did Charles Bronson portray in the series *Man with a Camera?*

474) Who was Miss Brooks's landlord in the sitcom *Our Miss Brooks?*

475) What were the names of Porter Ricks's two children in the adventure series *Flipper?*

476) Florence Halop portrayed this character in the sitcom *Meet Millie.*

. . . Answers

465. *Juvenile Jury*

466. Robert Stack

467. Pat Conway

468. Dr. San Rinehart

469. Mingo

470. Robert Young

471. Circle J Ranch

472. a. Feminum

473. Mike Kovac

474. Mrs. Margaret Davis

475. Sandy and Bud

476. Mama Bronson

477) What actress portrayed Jeannie in the sitcom *I Dream of Jeannie?*

478) What was the name of the suspense series in which a pair of eyes marked the beginning of each episode, followed by a bloody hand reaching to turn out the lights?

479) In the sitcom *The Charlie Farrell Show*, who played Charlie Farrell?

480) What was the name of the comedy show in which various amateurs with questionable attributes were rated by a panel of three celebrities, each act being rated on a scale of one to ten?

481) What was the name of Abe's law clerk in the series *The Law and Mr. Jones?*

482) In this quiz show first telecast in 1967, Monty Hall would select his contestants from the studio audience who donned loud costumes in an effort to be chosen.

483) Ida Morgenstern was played by what actress in the sitcom *Rhoda?*

484) Arthur Falconetti of the drama series *Rich Man, Poor Man* was portrayed by which actor?

485) What was the name of George Baxter's brother in the sitcom *Hazel?*

486) In the sitcom *The Beverly Hillbillies*, what was the name of Milburn Drysdale's assistant?

487) Who was the sole survivor in the new management overhaul of employees at the TV station in the sitcom *The Mary Tyler Moore Show?*

. . . *Answers*

477. Barbara Eden

478. *Lights Out*

479. Charlie Farrell

480. *The Gong Show*

481. C.E. Carruthers

482. *Let's Make a Deal*

483. Nancy Walker

484. William Smith

485. Steve

486. Jane Hathaway

487. Ted Baxter

488) What was Nellybelle in the series *The Roy Rogers Show?*
    a. horse
    b. donkey
    c. rifle
    d. jeep

489) Patrick McGoohan played the character of John Drake in what series?

490) What was the street number of the Ricardos' and Mertzes' in the sitcom *I Love Lucy?*

491) What was the name of Zorro's chief foe in the western *Zorro?*

492) In *The Jackie Gleason Show: The American Scene Magazine,* what was the name of the sketch which involved two lovelorn tenement residents?

493) In the western *The Californians,* what character did Adam Kennedy portray?

494) Who walked with a limp in the western *Gunsmoke?*

495) In the detective drama *Barnaby Jones,* Barnaby returned to his career as a private investigator because his son wanted to pursue a medical career and wasn't interested in that business. True or False?

496) What actress portrayed Mindy McConnell in the sitcom *Mork & Mindy?*

497) What was the name of the sitcom in which Walter Brennan played the grandfather who walked with a limp?

498) Johnny Yuma in the series *The Rebel* was an ex-U.S. Marshal. True or False?

. . . Answers

488. d. jeep

489. *Secret Agent*

490. 623 East 68th Street in Manhattan

491. Monastario

492. "Agnes and Arthur"

493. Dion Patrick

494. Chester Goode

495. False, his son was murdered while investigating a case

496. Pam Dawber

497. *The Real McCoys*

498. False, he was an ex-Confederate soldier

499) Who raised Lucan in the adventure series *Lucan?*
a. bears
b. aliens
c. Indians
d. wolves

500) What actor portrayed Rev. Tom Holvak in the drama *The Family Holvak?*

501) In the sitcom *Bosom Buddies,* Billy Joel wrote its theme "My Life." True or False.

502) The cases dramatized in the series *Dragnet* originated from the files of a San Francisco police department. True of False?

503) What actor portrayed "The Incredible Hulk" in the adventure series *The Incredible Hulk?*

504) Kwai Chang Caine was descended from Chinese American parents in the series *Kung Fu.* True or False?

505) What was the name of Sock's basset hound in the sitcom *The People's Choice?*

506) In the series *Room 222,* who played the part of Alice Johnson?

507) What was the name of Helen Roper's dog in the sitcom *The Ropers?*

508) In the war drama *From Here to Eternity* what actor portrayed Master Sgt. Milt Warden?

509) What was the quiz show *Break the Bank* renamed in the fall of 1956?

. . . Answers

499. d. wolves

500. Glenn Ford

501. True

502. False, Los Angeles

503. Lou Ferrigno

504. True

505. Cleo

506. Karen Valentine

507. Muffin

508. William Devane

509. *Break the $250,000 Bank*

510) What was Ralph Hinckley's name changed to in the adventure series *The Greatest American Hero?*

511) Who portrayed Florida Evans in the sitcom *Good Times?*

512) What was the name of the object that emerged from the black box located inside the house of *The Addams Family?*
    a. Hand
    b. It
    c. Thing
    d. Fang

513) What character did Hal March portray in the sitcom *The George Burns and Gracie Allen Show?*

514) What was the name of the character played by Billy Crystal in the sitcom *Soap?*

515) What actor portrayed Hank Dearborn in the sitcom *Hank?*

516) The police series *McCloud* was one of the three original shows of the *NBC Mystery Movie* series. True or False?

517) Which of the following was *not* a ranch hand in the western *The High Chaparral?*
    a. Reno
    b. Pedro
    c. Joe
    d. Jose

518) In the western *Cimarron City,* Beth Purcell was a bar owner. True or False?

519) E.G. Marshall played Lawrence Preston in the courtroom drama *The Defenders.* True or False?

. . . Answers

510. "Mr. H." or "Mr. Henley"

511. Esther Rolle

512. c. Thing

513. Harry Morton

514. Jodie Dallas

515. Dick Kallman

516. True

517. d. Jose

518. False, she was a boardinghouse owner

519. True

520) What was the name of the movie star in the sitcom *Gilligan's Island?*

521) What type of rifle did Chuck Connors use in the western *The Rifleman?*

522) Who taught Al Mundy his thievish skills in the intrigue series *It Takes a Thief?*
   a. brother
   b. friend
   c. father
   d. himself

523) Inspector Lewis Erskine in the police drama *The F.B.I.* was portrayed by Efrem Zimbalist, Jr. True or False?

524) What were the names of Wyatt's two brothers in the western *The Life and Legend of Wyatt Earp?*

525) Timmy Anderson was the name of Dennis Mitchell's friend in the sitcom *Dennis the Menace*. True or False?

526) What actress portrayed Stella Barnes in the sitcom *The Joey Bishop Show?*

527) Bud was the oldest of the Anderson children in the sitcom *Father Knows Best*. True or False?

528) The Nelsons' real life home in Hollywood had many similarities to the Nelsons' home on the set of *The Adventures of Ozzie & Harriet*. True or False?

529) What character did Cliff Norton portray in the sitcom *It's About Time?*

530) Name the three shows that made up the nucleus for the *NBC Sunday Mystery Movie*.

. . . Answers

520. Ginger

521. Winchester

522. c. father

523. True

524. Virgil and Morgan

525. False, Tommy Anderson

526. Marlo Thomas

527. False, Betty Anderson

528. True

529. Boss

530. *Columbo, McMillan and Wife,* and *McCloud*

531) The set of this quiz show appeared as a huge tic-tac-toe board with a celebrity in each square.

532) Pie-throwing was a frequent occurrence in this childrens show hosted by this TV personality.

533) What was the name of the giant dog in the *Soupy Sales* show whose only visible part was his paw?
a. Black Tooth   c. White Fang
b. Herman the Hound   d. Panther Paw

534) Who did Hot Lips Houlihan marry in the sitcom M*A*S*H?

535) Tony Randall was Robinson Peepers in the sitcom *Mr. Peepers?* True or False?

536) Name the two old folks who sat rocking on the porch in *The Carol Burnett Show,* portrayed by Carol Burnett and Harvey Korman.

537) Admiral Harriman Nelson was the main character in this series.

538) The Jacksons made their network TV debut in an on-location segment of *Walt Disney* entitled "Disneyland After Dark" in April 1962. True or False?

539) Who portrayed the devoted assistant to Bob Collins in *Love That Bob* who later became the housekeeper for *The Brady Bunch?*

540) Name the three chipmunks of the cartoon *The Alvin Show.*

541) Richard Dawson was the Executive Producer of *The $1.98 Beauty Show*. True or False?

. . . Answers

531. *Hollywood Squares*

532. Soupy Sales

533. c. White Fang

534. Lt. Col. Donald Penobscott

535. False, Wally Cox

536. Mr. Tudball and Mrs. Wiggins

537. *Voyage to the Bottom of the Sea*

538. False, it was the TV debut of the Osmond Brothers

539. Ann B. Davis as "Shultzy"

540. Alvin, Simon and Theodore

541. False, Chuck Barris

542) The sitcom *My Favorite Husband* originated from a 1948 radio series which starred this actress as Liz Cooper.

543) *The Violators* was the name of the magazine in the adventure series *The Name of the Game*. True or False?

544) In *The Adventures of Superman* which was released in the fall of 1952, who played Superman/Clark Kent?

545) Merv Griffin emceed this quiz show from 1959 to 1960 in which a secret phrase was the basis of the show.
   a. *Don't Stop Now*
   b. *Carry On*
   c. *Whisper Down the Lane*
   d. *Keep Talking*

546) What is the Clampetts' word for food in *The Beverly Hillbillies?*

547) What was the name of the famous sister group of *The Lawrence Welk Show?*

548) Who was the character Ruth Buzzi portrayed in the sitcom *That Girl?*

549) In the western series *Tales of Wells Fargo* what character did Dale Robertson portray?

550) What was the name of the orphan who joined the Sherman household in the western *Laramie?*
   a. Mike
   b. Bo
   c. Tommy
   d. Billy

551) Who was the retired sailor who joined the Douglas household in the sitcom *My Three Sons?*

. . . *Answers*

542. Lucille Ball

543. False, *Crime Magazine*

544. George Reeves

545. d. *Keep Talking*

546. vittles

547. Lennon Sisters

548. Margie "Pete" Peterson

549. Jim Hardie

550. a. Mike (Williams)

551. Uncle Charley O'Casey

552) Det. Danny Williams was the leader of the Five-O group in the police series *Hawaii Five-O*. True or False?

553) What was the first episode of *I Love Lucy* entitled?

554) What were the engine, coal car and mail car known as on the series *Petticoat Junction?*

555) What was Dagwood's profession in the sitcom *Blondie?*
    a. plumber
    b. lawyer
    c. doctor
    d. architect

556) The sitcom *Broadside* was produced by the creator of *McHale's Navy*. Name him.

557) In the sitcom *Bridget Loves Bernie,* the Fitzgerald family owned the New York City delicatessen above which the Steinberg couple lived. True or False?

558) What was the name of the nurse who eventually married Chick Hennesey in the comedy series *Hennesey?*

559) What detective series received its name from a Miami telephone exchange?

560) What actor played Major "Willie" Williston in the series *Steve Canyon?*

561) How many actors portrayed the Lone Ranger in the western *The Lone Ranger?*
    a. one
    b. two
    c. three
    d. four

. . . Answers

552. False, Det. Steve McGarrett

553. "The Girls Want to Go to a Nightclub"

554. The Cannonball

555. d. architect

556. Edward J. Montagne

557. False, Bernie's parents, the Steinbergs, owned the deli

558. Martha Hale

559. *Surfside Six*

560. Jerry Paris

561. b. two, Clayton Moore and John Hart

562) Patch was the name of the Quests' miniature bulldog in the *Jonny Quest* cartoon series. True or False?

563) Name the producers of the game show *To Tell the Truth*.

564) Who played the part of Walter Andrews in *The Tycoon?*

565) The name of the institute where the doctors worked was named after its founder Dr. David Craig in the medical series *The New Doctors*. True or False?

566) What character did Roosevelt Grier play in the series *Daniel Boone?*

567) In the sitcom *The Many Loves of Dobie Gillis,* Dobie and Maynard enlisted in the Air Force. True or False?

568) James T. West, a character in the series *The Wild Wild West,* was played by what actor?

569) What was the name of the original assistant principal in the sitcom *Welcome Back, Kotter?*

570) What was the inhuman quality possessed by Mark Harris in the adventure series *Man From Atlantis?*
    a. ability to fly
    b. ability to disappear
    c. ability to remain under water for a prolonged period
    d. ability to go back into time

571) What former mouseketeer played the part of a foreign exchange student in the sitcom *Make Room for Daddy?*

572) In the cartoon series *The Flintstones* what was the name of the city in which the Flintstones lived?

. . . *Answers*

562. False, Bandit

563. Mark Goodson and Bill Todman

564. Walter Brennan

565. True

566. Gabe Cooper

567. False, the Army

568. Robert Conrad

569. Mr. Woodman

570. c. ability to remain under water for a prolonged period

571. Annette Funicello

572. Bedrock

573) What was the name of Mac's wife in the police series
McMillan and Wife?
    a. Kelly
    b. Sally
    c. Shelly
    d. Amy

574) What actor portrayed Capt. Tony Nelson in the sitcom *I
Dream of Jeannie?*

575) What was the name of Chester Riley's wife in the sitcom
The Life of Riley?

576) Who was the first host of the comedy variety show *Caval-
cade of Stars?*

577) Apartment 3B was the Goldbergs' house number in the
sitcom *The Goldbergs*. True or False?

578) What actress replaced Cloris Leachman as Ruth Martin
in the adventure series *Lassie?*

579) What was "Lumpy's" full name in the sitcom *Leave It to
Beaver?*
    a. Terrence Rutherford
    b. Alexander Rutherford
    c. Clarence Rutherford
    d. none of these

580) 1969 was the year of the final telecast of *The Lawrence
Welk Show*. True or False?

581) What did Tom and Rudy Jordache's father do for a living in the series *Rich Man, Poor Man?*

. . . Answers

573. b. Sally

574. Larry Hagman

575. Peg

576. Jack Carter

577. True

578. June Lockhart

579. c. Clarence Rutherford

580. False, 1971

581. He was a baker

582) Who was the comedian who ended his shows with "God Bless"?
   a. Red Buttons
   b. Phil Silvers
   c. Rodney Dangerfield
   d. Red Skelton

583) What character operated the one-man taxi service in the detective series *Hawaiian Eye?*

584) Who portrayed Bruce Wayne (Batman) in the *Batman* fantasy adventure?

585) What was the name of the television station in the sitcom *The Mary Tyler Moore Show?*
   a. WJR-TV
   b. WJV-TV
   c. WJM-TV
   d. WJS-TV

586) The telephone operator in *Rowan & Martin's Laugh-In* was portrayed by Ruth Buzzi. True or False?

587) What was the street address of Dennis in the sitcom *Dennis the Menace?*

588) What was the nickname for Don Diego de la Vega in a western series whose title is the same as this nickname?

589) "Love in Bloom" was the theme song of this comedy show.

590) In the science fiction series *Buck Rogers in the 25th Century,* Princess Draconia was the leader of the Draconians. True or False?

591) The Douglas's farm was located outside this town in the sitcom *Green Acres.*

. . . *Answers*

582. d. Red Skelton

583. Kim

584. Adam West

585. c. WJM-TV

586. False, Lily Tomlin

587. 627 Elm Street

588. "Zorro"

589. *The Jack Benny Show*

590. False, Princess Ardala

591. Hooterville

592) What was the name of Bentley Gregg's houseboy in the sitcom *Bachelor Father?*

593) Which of the following characters was *not* a member of The Monkees in the series *The Monkees?*
   a. Davy
   b. Mark
   c. Micky
   d. Peter

594) Which actress portrayed Kate McCoy in the series *The Real McCoys?*

595) Saturn II was the name of the Robinson's spaceship in the science fiction series *Lost in Space*. True or False?

596) In the sitcom *Family Affair* what actor portrayed Bill Davis?

597) In the newspaper drama *Big Town,* what was the name of the newspaper?

598) What was the name of the second housekeeper in the sitcom *The Doris Day Show?*

599) What was the name of Diana's young daughter in the sitcom *I'm a Big Girl Now?*
   a. Becky
   b. Beth
   c. Bessie
   d. Brenda

600) What actor portrayed Lt. Theo Kojak in the police series *Kojak?*

601) Cathy Lane was portrayed by Patty Duke Astin in the sitcom *The Patty Duke Show*. True or False?

. . . *Answers*

592. Peter Tong

593. b. Mark, Mike was the fourth member

594. Kathy Nolan

595. False, *Jupiter II*

596. Brian Keith

597. *The Illustrated Press*

598. Juanita

599. a. Becky

600. Telly Savalas

601. True

602) Name the series from which *The Ropers* was developed.

603) What was the name of the character portrayed by Kate Jackson in the series *The Rookies?*

604) On what island was the sitcom *The Flying Nun* set?

605) This actress was the only member of the original cast in *The Brady Bunch* who did not return to play in *The Brady Bunch Hour.*
    a. Florence Henderson
    b. Susan Olsen
    c. Ann B. Davis
    d. Eve Plumb

606) What actress portrayed Jane Miller in the sitcom *The Good Life?*

607) *The Addams Family* sitcom originated with cartoon characters. True or False?

608) What was the name of the luxury liner in the sitcom *The Gale Storm Show?*

609) Name the person known for "Editorials" on *The Smothers Brothers Comedy Hour.*

610) Who did Ken Berry portray in the sitcom *Mayberry R.F.D.?*

611) In what territory was the Cannon's ranch located in the western *The High Chaparral?*
    a. Arizona
    b. California
    c. Mexico
    d. Colorado

. . . *Answers*

602. *Three's Company*

603. Jill Danko

604. Puerto Rico

605. d. Eve Plumb

606. Donna Mills

607. True

608. *S. S. Ocean Queen*

609. Pat Paulsen

610. Sam Jones

611. a. Arizona

612) In the detective series *Charlie's Angels,* what was the name of Charlie Townsend's assistant who was always on hand to aid the girls?

613) Who was the original host of the western *Death Valley Days?*

614) Which actress portrayed Gidget in the sitcom *Gidget?*

615) What was the first name of Marshal Torrance in the western *The Rifleman?*

616) In the intrigue series *The Invisible Man* of 1958 to 1960, the actor portraying Dr. Peter Brady was never seen. True or False?

617) In the western *Empire* what character did Ryan O'Neal portray?

618) What position did Jim "Dog" Kelly attain in the western *The Life and Legend of Wyatt Earp?*
   a. governor
   b. mayor
   c. congressman
   d. councilman

619) What actor portrayed Lt. John Russo in the police drama *The Detectives, Starring Robert Taylor?*

620) How many children did Joe and Katie Wabash have in the sitcom *Joe's World?*

621) Which actress played Katy in the sitcom *The Farmer's Daughter?*

622) James A. Michener created the series *Adventures in Paradise.* True or False?

. . . *Answers*

612. John Bosley

613. Stanley Andrews, "The Old Ranger"

614. Sally Field

615. Micah

616. True

617. Tal Garret

618. b. mayor

619. Tige Andrews

620. five

621. Inger Stevens

622. True

623) Walter Cronkite succeeded John Daly as moderator in this quiz show of the early 1950's.

624) Who played the part of Cisco Kid in the 1950 western TV series *The Cisco Kid?*

625) What character often used this line: "One of these days, Alice, one of these days . . . Pow! Right in the kisser!"?

626) What color was the car used in *Starsky and Hutch?*
    a. black
    b. blue
    c. yellow
    d. red

627) On the *Here's Lucy* show, Lucy's last name was Carmichael. True or False?

628) Who was Mr. Ed's owner in the sitcom *Mr. Ed?*

629) Officer Anderson of the sitcom *Car 54, Where Are You?* was played by which actor/comedian?

630) What country gave the U.S. the schooner *Kiwi* in the series *The Wackiest Ship in the Army?*

631) What was the name of the character played by Doug McClure in the series *The Virginian?*

632) This stepson of Shirley Jones portrayed Keith Partridge in the sitcom *The Partridge Family.*

633) In the sitcom *All in the Family,* the Bunkers' neighbors, the Jeffersons, moved from Queens to which location?
    a. Manhattan
    b. Harlem
    c. the Bronx
    d. Long Island

. . . Answers

623. *It's News to Me*

624. Duncan Renaldo

625. Ralph Kramden, *The Honeymooners*

626. d. red

627. False, Carter

628. Wilbur Post

629. Nipsey Russel

630. New Zealand

631. Trampas

632. David Cassidy

633. a. Manhattan

634) What actor portrayed Dr. James Kildare in the drama *Dr. Kildare?*

635) Truck driver Will Chandler was a law school graduate in the series *Movin' On*. True or False?

636) Who was John Monroe's daughter in the sitcom *My World and Welcome to It?*

637) Who played Marshal James Butler Hickok in the western *The Adventures of Wild Bill Hickok?*

638) In the *King of Diamonds* crime series what actor portrayed John King?

639) What was the name of Morticia's pet in the sitcom *The Addams Family?*
     a. Kit Kat
     b. Cleopatra
     c. Aristotle
     d. Homer

640) Sam Buckhart was born a Sioux Indian in the western *Law of the Plainsman*. True or False?

641) In the detective series *Switch,* what actor played the character Frank McBride?

642) What was the name of the old ranch hand who appeared during the second season of the western *Lance?*

643) What was the name of the Douglas' family dog in the sitcom *My Three Sons?*

644) In the western *Have Gun Will Travel,* Paladin operated out of this hotel.
     a. Hotel Belle   c. Hotel Carlton
     b. Hotel Victoria   d. none of these

. . . Answers

634. Richard Chamberlain

635. True

636. Lydia

637. Guy Madison

638. Broderick Crawford

639. b. Cleopatra, a man-eating plant

640. False, he was born an Apache Indian

641. Eddie Albert

642. Jelly Hoskins

643. Tramp

644. c. Hotel Carlton

645) What was the name of the town in *Petticoat Junction?*

646) What actor portrayed Buddy Flower in the sitcom *Bringing Up Buddy?*

647) Who portrayed Hec Ramsey in the western *Hec Ramsey?*

648) Sherman Billingsley, the owner of this club, eventually hosted this talk show, whose set was located inside the club. Name the title of the show which also represents the name of the club.

649) By what other title was *The Stu Erwin Show* commonly known?

650) The Ingalls family moved from Kansas to Walnut Grove, Minnesota in the series *Little House on the Prairie.* True or False?

651) What was the name of Jonny's scientist father in the *Jonny Quest* cartoon series?

652) What was the name of the dog owned by Nick and Nora Charles in the series *The Thin Man?*

653) What actor portrayed Dr. Paul Hunter in the medical series *The New Doctors?*

654) Det. Lt. Dan August was portrayed by which actor in the series *Dan August?*
    a. Burt Lancaster
    b. Robert Urich
    c. John Wayne
    d. Burt Reynolds

655) In the beginning of the series *Mannix,* Joe Mannix was employed by this sophisticated detective firm.

. . . Answers

645. Hooterville

646. Frank Aletter

647. Richard Boone

648. *The Stork Club*

649. *The Trouble With Father*

650. True

651. Dr. Benton Quest

652. Asta

653. David Hartman

654. d. Burt Reynolds

655. Intertect

656) In the sitcom *Welcome Back, Kotter* who played Gabe Kotter?

657) Dagmar was the son of Mama and Papa Hansen in the comedy series *Mama*. True or False.

658) What was the name of the foreign exchange student portrayed by Annette Funicello in the series *Make Room for Daddy?*

659) What was the name of the Flintstones pet dinosaur in the cartoon series *The Flintstones?*

660) "Blue Star" was the theme song of this medical series of the mid 1950's.

661) How many Macahan children were there in the western *How the West Was Won?*
    a. two
    b. three
    c. four
    d. five

662) Who emceed the discussion series *Life Begins at Eighty?*

663) What was the name of the local bank in the sitcom *Carter Country?*

664) Who called "Yoo-hoo, Mrs. Bloom" in the sitcom *The Goldbergs?*

665) In the sitcom *The Girl With Something Extra* what actor portrays John Burton?

666) Joe Riley was the oldest of the three spotlighted rangers in the western *Laredo*. True or False?

. . . Answers

656. Gabriel Kaplan

657. False, daughter

658. Gina Minelli

659. Dino

660. Medic

661. c. four

662. Jack Barry

663. Burnside Savings & Loan

664. Molly Goldberg

665. John Davidson

666. False, Reese Bennett was the oldest

667) What character did James Farentino portray in the series *The Lawyers?*

668) Name the comedy show in which Clem Kadiddlehopper was a favorite character.

669) What was the name of the Baxter's son in the sitcom *Hazel?*
   a. Jim
   b. Harold
   c. Brian
   d. Walter

670) What was the name of the quiz show, first emceed by Bud Collyer, in which the contestants were chosen from the audience and given various stunts to perform within a given time limit?

671) What actor portrayed Mark Saber in *The Vise,* a detective series?

672) The horse on which Dale Evans rode in *The Roy Rogers Show* was called Bullet. True or False?

673) Who was the Ricardos' babysitter in the sitcom *I Love Lucy?*

674) What actor portrayed Prof. Le Blanc in *The Jack Benny Show?*

675) What actor portrayed Jody O'Connell in the western *Buckskin?*

676) What was the name of the saloon in the western *Gunsmoke?*

. . . Answers

667. Neil Darrell

668. *The Red Skelton Show*

669. b. Harold

670. *Beat the Clock*

671. Donald Gray

672. False, it was called Buttermilk

673. Mrs. Trumbull

674. Mel Blanc

675. Tommy Nolan

676. Longbranch Saloon

677) What was the flyers squadron number in the war drama
Baa Baa Black Sheep?
   a. 333
   b. 878
   c. 214
   d. none of these

678) Which musician portrayed Mike in the sitcom *The
Monkees?*

679) What was the name of the leading character in the western *The Rebel?*

680) This young Robinson boy was frequently seen with the
Robot in the science fiction series *Lost in Space.*

681) Who was the owner-publisher of the *Los Angeles Tribune*
in the series *Lou Grant?*

682) In the sitcom *Bewitched,* Esmerelda was the name of the
Stephens' first child. True or False?

683) In the sitcom *The Doris Day Show* what was the name of
Doris Martin's father?

684) What actor portrayed Alexander Scott in the adventure
series *I Spy?*

685) This children's show featured the puppets of Burr Till-
strom and was hosted by Fran Allison.

686) Patty Lane's intellectual cousin was from this country in
the sitcom *The Patty Duke Show.*
   a. England
   b. Scotland
   c. Finland
   d. Norway

. . . *Answers*

677. c. 214

678. Mike Nesmith

679. Johnny Yuma

680. Will Robinson

681. Margaret Pynchon

682. False, Tabitha

683. Buck

684. Bill Cosby

685. *Kukla, Fran & Ollie*

686. b. Scotland

687) What was the name of the police show which featured officers Webster, Gillis and Danko?

688) What was the name of the Puerto Rican nun in the sitcom *The Flying Nun?*

689) Tiger was the name of the family dog in the sitcom *The Brady Bunch*. True or False?

690) What was the name of Bert's diner in the sitcom *The Good Guys?*

691) In the fall of which year did *The Addams Family* make its debut?

692) Who was the narrator in the series *The Fugitive?*

693) Other than his niece Penny, which other relative of Sky King's lived on the ranch with him in the series *Sky King?*

694) What actor portrayed Bart's friend Dandy Jim Buckley in the western *Maverick?*

695) What was the name of Big John's son in the western *The High Chaparral?*

696) Louie the garbageman was played by which actor in the sitcom *Chico and the Man?*

697) Who hosted *Death Valley Days* from 1965-1966?

698) What was the name of the cottage in the sitcom *The Ghost and Mrs. Muir?*
    a. Gull Cottage
    b. Sea Cottage
    c. Love Cottage
    d. Green Cottage

. . . Answers

687. *The Rookies*

688. Sister Sixto

689. True

690. Bert's Place

691. 1964

692. William Conrad

693. Clipper, his nephew

694. Efrem Zimbalist, Jr.

695. Billy Blue

696. Scatman Crothers

697. Ronald Reagan

698. a. Gull Cottage

699) Name the actress who originally portrayed the voice of "Sam" in the detective series *Richard Diamond, Private Detective*.

700) What was the name of the young orphaned clerk in the western *The Iron Horse?*
    a. Barnabas
    b. Barabas
    c. Benjamin
    d. Benedict

701) In the series *Emergency* what were the names of the two paramedics?

702) After leaving Dodge City, Wyatt moved to this Arizona town in the western *The Life and Legend of Wyatt Earp*.

703) Buddy Sorrell was portrayed by Morey Amsterdam in the sitcom *The Dick Van Dyke Show*. True or False?

704) What was the name of Joe Forrester's girlfriend in the police series *Joe Forrester?*

705) In the sitcom *Father Knows Best* what actor portrayed Jim Anderson?

706) Who was TV's first Ellery Queen?

707) What were the names of the two astronauts stranded in the Stone Age in the sitcom *It's About Time?*
    a. Larry and Bud
    b. Roger and Rex
    c. Hector and Mac
    d. Alan and Max

708) Who portrayed Cheyenne Bodie in the western *Cheyenne?*

. . . Answers

699. Mary Tyler Moore

700. a. Barnabas

701. Roy DeSoto and John Gage

702. Tombstone

703. True

704. Georgia Cameron

705. Robert Young

706. Richard Hart

707. c. Hector and Mac

708. Clint Walker

709) Who hosted the talent show *Hollywood Screen Test* following the departure of Bert Lytell?

710) In the series *Star Trek,* Mr. Spock's pointed ears were a characteristic from this planet.

711) What is the name of Sonny and Cher's child who appeared at the conclusion of each show of *The Sonny and Cher Comedy Hour?*

712) What actor portrayed Maj. Frank Burns in the sitcom M*A*S*H?

713) Who was the original leader of the Impossible Missions Force in the intrigue series *Mission: Impossible?*

714) Joseph Armagh's wealth was attained through investments in the oil industry in the drama *Captains and the Kings.* True or False?

715) Who played "The Virginian" in the series of the same name?

716) This series was ABC's first major hit, first telecast in 1954.

717) What was the name of the authoritative professor in the series *The Paper Chase?*

718) What was the new name of the sitcom *All in the Family* which was changed in the fall of 1979?

719) Who were the two intern friends of Dr. James Kildare in the drama *Dr. Kildare?*

. . . *Answers*

709. Neil Hamilton

710. Vulcan

711. Chastity

712. Larry Linville

713. Daniel Briggs

714. True

715. James Drury

716. *Disneyland*

717. Professor Charles W. Kingsfield, Jr.

718. *Archie Bunker's Place*

719. Dr. Simon Agurski and Dr. Thomas Gerson

20) What rock star performed "Crocodile Rock" on *The Muppet Show?*
  a. Mick Jagger
  b. Rod Stewart
  c. Chuck Berry
  d. Elton John

21) What actor portrayed a Samurai warrior on NBC's *Saturday Night Live?*

22) In *The Adventures of Superman,* the only time Superman became vulnerable was in the presence of this element.

23) What was the name of the song which was sung by the entire King family at the conclusion of each telecast in *The King Family Show?*

24) Hound was the name of the Clampetts' dog in *The Beverly Hillbillies.* True or False?

25) Peter Brown portrayed this character in the western *The Lawman.*

26) These two rangers were the main characters in the *Tales of the Texas Rangers*.

27) What was Jack Jackson's nickname in the series *That's My Boy?*

28) What was the name of Barry Lockridge's dog in the science fiction series *Land of the Giants?*

29) J.J. of the sitcom *The Governor & J.J.* worked in a chocolate factory. True or False?

30) Which actress portrayed stewardess Betty Hamilton in the science fiction series *Land of the Giants?*

. . . Answers

720. d. Elton John

721. John Belushi

722. Kryptonite

723. "Love at Home"

724. False, Duke

725. Deputy Johnny McKay

726. Ranger Jace Pearson and Ranger Clay Morgan

727. Jarring

728. Chipper

729. False, aside from serving as first lady she worked in a zoo

730. Heather Young

731) What did Tim O'Hara of the sitcom *My Favorite Martian* do for a living?

732) In the detective series *Harry-O* what character was portrayed by David Janssen?

733) What was the name of the character portrayed by Phil Silvers on *The Phil Silvers Show: You'll Never Get Rich?*

734) It was the duty of Tom Jeffords of the western *Broken Arrow* to safely deliver which of the following through Apache territory?
   a. gold
   b. mail
   c. military orders
   d. money

735) Richard Benjamin portrayed Dick Hollister in the sitcom *He & She*. True or False?

736) What was the character name of actor Van Williams in the series *Surfside Six?*

737) What was the name of the educated mayor's son in the police series *Lobo?*

738) Mother Maybelle & The Carter Family were regulars in this musical variety show.

739) What was the name of the sheriff in the western *Tombstone Territory?*

740) What actress portrayed Jenny Preston in the sitcom *The New Dick Van Dyke Show?*

741) Daniel Boone had two children in the TV series *Daniel Boone*. True or False?

. . . Answers

731. newspaper reporter

732. Harry Orwell

733. Sgt. Ernie Bilko

734. b. mail

735. True

736. Ken Madison

737. Deputy Birdie Hawkins

738. *The Johnny Cash Show*

739. Sheriff Clay Hollister

740. Hope Lange

741. True, Jemima, daughter and Israel, son

742) Who did Victor Jory portray in the police series *Manhunt?*

743) Dick Van Patten portrayed this character in the comedy series *Mama.*

744) Who played the part of Freddie "Boom Boom" Washington in the sitcom *Welcome Back, Kotter?*

745) Miss Brooks's first romantic interest revolved around this shy biology teacher in the sitcom *Our Miss Brooks.*

746) In the sitcom *Fish,* the Fish couple became foster parents to how many kids?
    a. two
    b. three
    c. four
    d. five

747) Millie Bronson of the sitcom *Meet Millie* was portrayed by this actress.

748) In the intrigue series *The Hunter* who first portrayed Bart Adams?

749) What was the name of the undertaker in the early episodes of the sitcom *The Life of Riley?*

750) Which of the Cartwrights did Dan Blocker portray in the western *Bonanza?*

751) In the sitcom *The Girl With Something Extra,* what was the "extra" possessed by Sally Burton?
    a. money
    b. vitality
    c. E.S.P.
    d. superhuman powers

. . . Answers

742. Det. Lt. Howard Finucane

743. Nels

744. Lawrence-Hilton Jacobs

745. Mr. Boynton

746. d. five

747. Elena Verdugo

748. Barry Nelson

749. Digby "Digger" O'Dell

750. "Hoss" Cartwright

751. c. E.S.P.

752) What was the name of the couple to whom Ellen Miller sold her farm in the adventure series *Lassie?*

753) What were the names of Beaver's parents in the sitcom *Leave It to Beaver?*

754) Name the mute hobo played by Red Skelton in the series *The Red Skelton Show.*

755) This actor portrayed Tracy Steele in the detective series *Hawaiian Eye.*

756) In the medical drama *Ben Casey,* what doctor replaced Dr. David Zorba as Chief of Surgery?

757) In the detective series *Martin Kane, Private Eye,* Martin Kane spent much of his time in this tobacco shop.

758) What signified the conclusion of each episode of *Rowan & Martin's Laugh-In?*
    a. announcer's farewell
    b. hysterical laugh
    c. clash of cymbals
    d. a pair of hands clapping

759) Felix Unger moved out of the apartment to marry his girlfriend Miriam in the sitcom *The Odd Couple.* True or False?

760) What was the name of Jack Paar's daughter in *The Jack Paar Program?*

761) In the science fiction series *Buck Rogers,* what actor replaced Kem Dibbs as Buck Rogers in this first TV version?

762) What actor portrayed Oliver Wendell Douglas in the sitcom *Green Acres?*

. . . Answers

752. Ruth and Paul Martin

753. June and Ward Cleaver

754. Freddie the Freeloader

755. Anthony Eisley

756. Dr. Daniel Freeland

757. Happy McMann's

758. d. a pair of hands clapping

759. False, he moved to marry his ex-wife Gloria

760. Randy

761. Robert Pastene

762. Eddie Albert

763) In the war drama *Baa Baa Black Sheep*, who portrayed Maj. Gregory "Pappy" Boyington?

764) What captain in the police series *The Mod Squad* was responsible for the formation of the youth squad?

765) What was the name of Luke McCoy's wife in the series *The Real McCoys?*

766) In the drama *Family* Doug Lawrence was a chemical engineer. True or False?

767) What actor portrayed Lou Grant in the series *Lou Grant?*

768) Patrick McVey and Mark Stevens both played this editor in the newspaper drama *Big Town.*

769) Who played the piece of music composed by Richard Nixon on *The Jack Paar Program?*
   a. Jack Paar
   b. Miriam Paar
   c. Richard Nixon
   d. Randy Paar

770) What was the name of the club which employed Ricky Ricardo in *I Love Lucy?*

771) Det. Stavros was portrayed by George Savalas, who was billed under what name during the first two seasons of the police series *Kojak?*

772) Who was Sock's freeloading buddy in the sitcom *The People's Choice?*

773) What was the name of the high school in which Homeroom 222 was located in the series *Room 222?*

. . . Answers

763. Robert Conrad

764. Capt. Adam Greer

765. Kate McCoy

766. False, a lawyer

767. Edward Asner

768. Steve Wilson

769. c. Richard Nixon

770. The Tropicana

771. Demosthenes

772. Rollo

773. Walt Whitman High

774) Tennessee Ernie Ford was a regular in the musical variety show, *The Ford Show*. True or False?

775) What was the name of the Brady's housekeeper in the sitcom *The Brady Bunch?*

776) In the adventure series *The Greatest American Hero*, why was character Ralph Hinkley's name changed?

777) Kent McCord portrayed this rookie officer in the series *Adam 12*.

778) Bob Emery, also known as "Big Brother," hosted which children's TV show during the late 40's and early 1950's?
   a. *Small Fry Club*
   b. *Sleepy Joe*
   c. *Happy the Clown*
   d. *Capt. Kangaroo*

779) What was the name of Susanna Pomeroy's friend in the sitcom *The Gale Storm Show?*

780) What actor portrayed Sam McCloud in the police series *McCloud?*

781) High Chaparral was the name given to the ranch owned by the Cannons in the western *The High Chaparral*. True or False?

782) What actor portrayed Chico Rodriguez in the sitcom *Chico and the Man?*

783) In the sitcom *December Bride,* what was the name of Lily Ruskin's daughter?

784) What was the name of the U.S. intelligence agency that Maxwell Smart and Susan Hilton worked for in the sitcom *Get Smart?*

. . . Answers

774. True

775. Alice Nelson

776. Because of the assassination attempt on Reagan's life by John Hinckley

777. Officer Jim Reed

778. a. *Small Fry Club*

779. Esmerelda "Nugey" Nugent

780. Dennis Weaver

781. True

782. Freddie Prinze

783. Ruth Henshaw

784. C.O.N.T.R.O.L.

785) Name the show in which Chuck Connors played Lucas McCain.

786) Who portrayed Ben Calhoun in the western *The Iron Horse?*

787) Who was the assistant to the FBI director in the police drama *The F.B.I.?*
   a. Arthur Warner
   b. Arthur Ward
   c. Arthur Wood
   d. Arthur Wayne

788) Who was the handpicked sheriff of Old Man Clanton in the western *The Life and Legend of Wyatt Earp?*

789) What character did Allen Case portray in the western *The Deputy?*

790) In the second season of *The Joey Bishop Show*, Joey was depicted as a nightclub entertainer. True or False?

791) What was the name of the town in which the sitcom *Father Knows Best* was set?

792) In this adventure series, the last name of the main character is synonymous with the weapon that he uses.

793) What was the name of Janis Stewart's daughter in the sitcom *It's Always Jan?*

794) The short story "The Caballero's Way" by O. Henry was the foundation from which *The Cisco Kid* series was based. True or False?

795) What actor portrayed Ed Norton in the sitcom *The Honeymooners?*

. . . Answers

785. *The Rifleman*

786. Dale Robertson

787. b. Arthur Ward

788. Johnny Behan

789. Clay McCord

790. False, he was the host of a talk show

791. Springfield

792. *Bowie*

793. Josie

794. True

795. Art Carney

796) What was the character name of Starsky and Hutch's captain in the series *Starsky and Hutch?*

797) Who composed the jazzy "Theme from M Squad" of the police series *M Squad?*

798) Who was the talking horse in this sitcom of the early 1960's?

799) Who portrayed Joseph Armagh in the drama *Captains and the Kings?*

800) What was the character name given to the cook in the western *Wagon Train?*

801) What character did James Stephens portray in the series *The Paper Chase?*

802) Whose voice was that of the three chipmunks and David Seville in the cartoon *The Alvin Show?*

803) What was the last name of the Italian couple who became neighbors to the Bunkers in the sitcom *All in the Family?*

804) What was the name of the comedy show, hosted by Don Adams, which matched pre-selected studio contestants with guest stars for the re-enactment of famous movie scenes?

805) Who was the only character who appeared normal in the sitcom *The Munsters?*

806) Where was the "Naked City" of the police series *Naked City?*
   a. Chicago
   b. Los Angeles
   c. San Francisco
   d. New York

. . . Answers

796. Capt. Harold Dobey

797. Count Basie

798. Mr. Ed

799. Richard Jordan

800. Charley Wooster

801. James T. Hart

802. Ross Bagdasarian

803. Lorenzo

804. *Don Adams' Screen Test*

805. Marilyn Munster

806. d. New York

807) Who made Superman's costume in *The Adventures of Superman?*

808) What actor portrayed Seldom Jackson in the comedy series *Kentucky Jones?*

809) Capt. Binghamton of *McHale's Navy* referred to McHale's men as a crew of thieves. True or False?

810) What decade was portrayed in the police series *The Lawless Years?*
    a. 1920's
    b. 1930's
    c. 1940's
    d. 1950's

811) Who played the part of Don Hollinger in the sitcom *That Girl?*

812) What were the names of the two brothers who inherited the ranch subsequent to their father's death in the western *Laramie?*

813) What was the name of Irma's first boyfriend who was replaced by Joe Vance in the sitcom *My Friend Irma?*

814) Paladin of the western *Have Gun Will Travel* was educated at West Point. True or False?

815) Who played the handyman in *The Stu Erwin Show* and also on *My Little Margie?*

816) What actress played Lt. Anne Morgan in the sitcom *Broadside?*

817) What actor portrayed Seaman Shatz in the comedy series *Hennesey?*

. . . *Answers*

807. his mother, Mrs. Sarah Kent

808. Harry Morgan

809. False, a crew of pirates

810. a. 1920's

811. Ted Bessell

812. Slim and Andy Sherman

813. Al

814. True

815. Willie Best

816. Kathy Nolan

817. Arte Johnson

818) In the detective series *Surfside Six,* what actor played the part of Sandy Winfield II?

819) The Lone Ranger's income was derived from a mine which yielded this resource in the western *The Lone Ranger.*
   a. silver
   b. gold
   c. diamonds
   d. coal

820) Which black female singer portrayed Julia in the sitcom *Julia?*

821) Who played the part of Michael Endicott in the series *To Rome With Love?*

822) What was the name of Dick Preston's sister in the sitcom *The New Dick Van Dyke Show?*

823) What was the name of Daniel Boone's wife in the TV series *Daniel Boone?*

824) Bob Denver portrayed this character in the sitcom *The Many Loves of Dobie Gillis.*

825) Which actress portrayed Mama in the comedy series *Mama?*

826) Name the game show in which the panelists tried to identify the contestant's occupation.

827) In the series *Make Room for Daddy* what was the name of the club where Danny Williams performed?

828) In the cartoon series *The Flintstones* a baby elephant with a long trunk was used as the Flintstones' vacuum cleaner. True or False?

. . . Answers

818. Troy Donahue

819. a. silver

820. Diahann Carroll

821. John Forsythe

822. "Mike"

823. Rebecca Boone

824. Maynard G. Krebs

825. Peggy Wood

826. *What's My Line*

827. The Copa Club

828. True

829) Who was Stewart and Sally McMillan's maid in the police series *McMillan and Wife?*

830) What was the name of the aunt in the western *How the West Was Won?*
   a. Aunt Polly
   b. Aunt Molly
   c. Aunt Holly
   d. Aunt Dolly

831) What character of a situation comedy was known for this phrase: "What a revoltin' development this is!"

832) What actor portrayed Adam Cartwright in the western *Bonanza?*

833) What was the name of the theme song in the musical variety show *The Glen Campbell Goodtime Hour?*

834) In the series *The Law and Mr. Jones,* what was the full name of Mr. Jones?

835) *The Lawrence Welk Show* ran for 16 years on NBC. True or False?

836) What actress portrayed Rhoda Morgenstern Gerard in the sitcom *Rhoda?*

837) Connie Stevens portrayed this singer-photographer in the detective series *Hawaiian Eye.*

838) What state was the oil found in the sitcom *The Beverly Hillbillies?*

839) Who did Ted Baxter marry in the sitcom *The Mary Tyler Moore Show?*

. . . *Answers*

829. Mildred

830. b. Aunt Molly

831. Chester A. Riley

832. Pernell Roberts

833. "Gentle on My Mind"

834. Abraham Lincoln Jones

835. False, ABC

836. Valerie Harper

837. Cricket Blake

838. Tennessee

839. Georgette Franklin

840) In the series *Run for Your Life*, Paul Bryan had which of the following?

    a. an incurable disease
    b. a heart attack
    c. a broken leg
    d. a skull fracture

841) Jack Klugman's real wife portrayed his ex-wife in the sitcom *The Odd Couple*. Who was the actress and what character did she portray?

842) What was the name of the Longbranch Saloon's first manager in the western *Gunsmoke?*

843) The Draconians discovered Buck Rogers's spacecraft in which year in the science fiction series *Buck Rogers in the 25th Century?*

    a. 1491
    b. 2491
    c. 3491
    d. 4491

844) Ken Berry starred in this show which became the successor to *The Andy Griffith Show*.

845) Tige Andrews portrayed Pete Cochran in the police series *The Mod Squad*. True or False?

846) Who played Johnny Yuma in the series *The Rebel?*

847) Letitia "Buddy" Lawrence was played by which actress in the drama *Family?*

848) What actress portrayed Jane Foster in the series *East Side/West Side?*

849) In the western *The Big Valley*, who played Heath Barkley?

. . . Answers

840. a. an incurable disease

841. Brett Somers - Blanche

842. Kitty Russell

843. b. 2491

844. *Mayberry, R.F.D.*

845. False, Michael Cole portrayed Pete

846. Nick Adams

847. Kristy McNichol

848. Cicely Tyson

849. Lee Majors

850) The phrase "Just the facts, Ma'am" was popularized by this police drama.

851) Which of the following characterizations was *not* portrayed in *The Jackie Gleason Show?*
    a. The Poor Soul
    b. Reggie Van Gleason III
    c. Fenwick Babbitt
    d. Clumsy Claude

852) What were the names of the Ricardo's landlords in *I Love Lucy?*

853) Karate and Judo were derived from this martial art which was also the name of a philosophical Western.

854) Who was Perry Mason's personal investigator in the series *Perry Mason?*

855) Who played Lt. Eddie Ryker in the police series *The Rookies?*

856) In *The Fred Waring Show* what was the title of the dance contest?

857) What was the name of the comedy variety series which succeeded *The Brady Bunch?*

858) What was the name of Florida Evans's neighbor and friend in the sitcom *Good Times?*

859) From whom did *The Addams Family* sitcom receive its name?

860) What actor portrayed Buck Cannon in the western *The High Chaparral?*

850. *Dragnet*

851. d. Clumsy Claude

852. Fred and Ethel Mertz

853. Kung Fu

854. Paul Drake

855. Gerald S. O'Loughlin

856. "Video Ballroom"

857. *The Brady Bunch Hour*

858. Willona Woods

859. Charles Addams

860. Cameron Mitchell

861) Walter Findlay was Maude's fourth husband in the sitcom *Maude*. True or False?

862) Where did the name T & T Circus originate in the drama *Frontier Circus?*

863) In the sitcom *Soap,* what actor played the part of Benson?

864) The theme song "Chico and the Man" of the sitcom *Chico and the Man* was written and performed by Jose Feliciano. True or False?

865) What actress portrayed Mrs. Margaret Williams in the sitcom *The Danny Thomas Show?*

866) What was the agent number of Susan Hilton in the sitcom *Get Smart?*

867) Name the actor who played the marshal in the western series *The Rifleman.*

868) Other than Gilligan and "The Skipper," how many passengers had been stranded on *Gilligan's Island?*

869) What was the name of the first policewoman in the police series *Ironside?*

870) Wyatt's friend Jim Kelly was better known under this name in the western *The Life and Legend of Wyatt Earp.*

871) What actor portrayed Dr. Joe Early in the series *Emergency?*

872) Who was the neighbor of Dennis Mitchell in the sitcom *Dennis the Menace?*

. . . Answers

861. True

862. Col. Casey Thompson and Ben Travis

863. Robert Guillaume

864. True

865. Jean Hagen

866. Agent 99

867. Paul Fix

868. five

869. Eve Whitfield

870. Jim "Dog" Kelly

871. Bobby Troup

872. George Wilson

873) What was the name of Jim Henson's muppet hound in *The Jimmy Dean Show?*

874) What was the name of the congressman in the sitcom *The Farmer's Daughter?*
   a. Glen Morley
   b. Edward Stevens
   c. George Kane
   d. Richard Evans

875) Name the actor who portrayed Captain Adam Troy in the series *Adventures in Paradise.*

876) *It's a Living* is a sitcom based on the lives of four waitresses. True or False?

877) What was the name of the original undercover agent in the western series *Colt .45?*

878) What actor portrayed Col. Wilhelm Klink in the sitcom *Hogan's Heroes?*

879) What character did George Takei play in the series *Star Trek?*

880) Who was Lt. Frank Ballinger's commanding officer in the police series *M Squad?*

881) What subject did John Novak teach in the series *Mr. Novak?*
   a. History
   b. Science
   c. Mathematics
   d. English

882) Who played Eunice's younger sister Chrissy in *The Carol Burnett Show?*

. . . Answers

873. Rowlf

874. a. Glen Morley

875. Gardner McKay

876. False, there are five waitresses

877. Christopher Colt

878. Werner Klemperer

879. Sulu

880. Capt. Grey

881. d. English

882. Vicki Lawrence

883) What was the name of the schooner used in the series *The Wackiest Ship in the Army?*

884) Who was Bob Collins's nephew in the sitcom *Love That Bob* who went on to star as Dobie Gillis?

885) What was the name of Donna's husband in the sitcom *The Donna Reed Show?*

886) What character did Yvonne DeCarlo portray in the sitcom *The Munsters?*

887) What was the newscaster name of Gilda Radner on NBC's *Saturday Night Live?*

888) In *The Adventures of Superman* the natural parents of Clark Kent sent him to Earth in a rocket which landed in which American town?
   a. Cedar Rock
   b. Summit Hill
   c. Smallville
   d. Hooterville

889) This musical variety show of the late 1960's featured a score of family members including sisters, brothers, husbands, cousins and kids.

890) Who did Allison Mackenzie marry in the soap *Peyton Place?*

891) The police series *The Lawless Years* was set in the city of Chicago. True or False?

892) In the western *Laramie* what was the name of the drifter who joined the Sherman ranch?

893) The home of Ann Marie's parents was located in this city and state in the sitcom *That Girl.*

. . . Answers

883. *Kiwi*

884. Dwayne Hickman

885. Alex

886. Lily Munster

887. Rosanne Rosanna-Dana

888. c. Smallville

889. *The King Family Show*

890. Rodney Harrington

891. False, New York City

892. Jess Harper

893. Brewster, New York

894) Who was Irma Peterson's boss in the sitcom *My Friend Irma?*

895) What was the name of the Oriental worker in the western *Have Gun Will Travel?*

896) What were the names of the ghosts in the series *Topper?*

897) What was the name of the railroad on *Petticoat Junction?*

898) What actress portrayed Dr. Margaret Kleeb in the sitcom *The Brothers?*

899) In what town was the comedy series *Here Come the Brides* set?
   a. Boston
   b. Philadelphia
   c. Seattle
   d. San Francisco

900) Who was the spokesperson for the commercials aired by Westinghouse during the *Studio One* telecasts?

901) Before he became the Lone Ranger, John Reid was his name in the western *The Lone Ranger.* True or False?

902) Who did Steve Bruce replace in Julia's love life in the sitcom *Julia?*

903) Who hosted the show *This is Your Life?*

904) What was the name of the officer in the cartoon series *Top Cat?*

. . . Answers

894. Mr. Clyde

895. Hey Boy

896. Marian and George Kirby

897. C.F. & W. Railroad

898. Ann Morriss

899. c. Seattle

900. Betty Furness

901. True

902. Paul Cameron

903. Ralph Edwards

904. Office Dribble

905) What was the name of the soap opera series in which Dick Preston acquired a role as Dr. Brad Fairmont in the sitcom *The New Dick Van Dyke Show?*
    a. *Those Who Dare*
    b. *Those Who Pair*
    c. *Those Who Love*
    d. *Those Who Care*

906) What was the profession of Tom Corbett in the show *The Courtship of Eddie's Father?*

907) In the police series *Manhunt,* Ben Andrews was a detective. True or False?

908) What actor portrayed Mike Barnett in the detective series *Man Against Crime?*

909) Which insurance company sponsored the show *Wild Kingdom?*

910) What character did Richard Crenna portray in the sitcom *Our Miss Brooks?*

911) What was the last name of the Flintstones' neighbors in the cartoon series *The Flintstones?*

912) What actor portrayed Dr. Konrad Styner in the series *Medic?*

913) Ed Norton worked in the sewers of New York City in the sitcom *The Honeymooners.* True or False?

914) What were the names of the Riley's two children in the sitcom *The Life of Riley?*

915) Who played Little Joe Cartwright in the western *Bonanza?*

. . . Answers

905. d. *Those Who Care*

906. magazine publisher

907. False, a reporter

908. Ralph Bellamy

909. Mutual of Omaha

910. Walter Denton

911. Rubble

912. Richard Boone

913. True

914. Babs and Junior

915. Michael Landon

916) What did Gomer Pyle do for a living before he signed up in the Marines Corps in the sitcom *Gomer Pyle, U.S.M.C.?*

917) What actor portrayed "Gramps" Miller in the adventure series *Lassie?*

918) What was the name of the law firm in the series *The Lawyers?*

919) What was the name of the doorman in the sitcom *Rhoda?*

920) Who played the part of Maggie Porter in *Rich Man, Poor Man — Book II?*

921) What hotel served as a base for Tom Lopaka and Tracy Steele in the detective series *Hawaiian Eye?*

922) In the sitcom *Barney Miller,* what was the name of the old cop who eventually got his own series?

923) This character was the contact on the Honolulu police force in the detective series *Hawaiian Eye.*

924) What producer created the soap *Mary Hartman, Mary Hartman?*

925) What do the initials S.W.A.T. stand for in the series of the same name?

926) What was the name of Roy Rogers's horse in the series *The Roy Rogers Show?*

927) What was the apartment of the "Odd Couple" in the sitcom *The Odd Couple?*
    a. 1002
    b. 1018
    c. 1028
    d. 1038

. . . Answers

916. gas station attendant

917. George Cleveland

918. Nichols, Darrell & Darrell

919. Carlton

920. Susan Sullivan

921. Hawaiian Village Hotel

922. Det. Phil Fish

923. Quon

924. Norman Lear

925. Special Weapons and Tactics

926. Trigger

927. a. Apartment 1002

928) What was the name of the nightclub owner portrayed by Dick Powell in the drama *Four Star Playhouse?*

929) In what state was the western *Gunsmoke* set?
    a. Nebraska
    b. Kansas
    c. Arizona
    d. Illinois

930) Who was responsible for all the voices in the cartoon *The Bugs Bunny Show?*

931) What was the name of Andy Taylor's son in the sitcom *The Andy Griffith Show?*

932) The Monkees were chosen for the sitcom *The Monkees* because of their hit singles and overall popularity with teenagers. True or False?

933) What was the name of Luke McCoy's younger brother in *The Real McCoys?*

934) Who played the character "The Range Rider" in the western *The Range Rider?*

935) What was the name of Bill Davis's gentleman housekeeper in the sitcom *Family Affair?*

936) In the sitcom *Love on a Rooftop*, David Willis was an intern. True or False?

937) In the sitcom *The Bob Newhart Show,* what character does Suzanne Pleshette portray?

938) What was the name of Dave Kelsey's wife in the sitcom *The Donna Reed Show?*

. . . Answers

928. Willie Dante

929. b. Kansas

930. Mel Blanc

931. Opie

932. False, The Monkees did not previously exist but were "manufactured" for the part.

933. Little Luke

934. Jock Mahoney

935. Mr. French

936. False, he was an apprentice architect

937. Emily Hartley

938. Midge

939) What comedian popularized the phrase "How sweet it is!"?

940) Who sang the theme song "I'm a Big Girl Now" in the sitcom of the same name?

941) What actress portrayed Ethel Mertz in the *I Love Lucy* show?

942) What was the name of the plainclothesman who assisted Kojak in the series *Kojak?*

943) What actor portrays Socrates Miller in the sitcom *The People's Choice?*

944) What was the name of Flo Castleberrys' bar in the sitcom *Flo?*
   a. Flo's Pink Rose
   b. Flo's Yellow Rose
   c. Flo's Red Rose
   d. Flo's White Rose

945) In the sitcom *The Brady Bunch* what was the name of the oldest son?

946) In the sitcom *Good Times* what character popularized the phrase "Dy-No-Mite"?

947) What was the name of the character in *The Addams Family* famous for the words "You Rang?"

948) What actor portrayed Big John Cannon in the western *The High Chaparral?*

949) Following James Garner's departure from the western *Maverick* what character entered the series?

. . . Answers

939. Jackie Gleason

940. Diana Canova

941. Vivian Vance

942. Bobby Crocker

943. Jackie Cooper

944. b. Flo's Yellow Rose

945. Greg Brady

946. James Evans, Jr. or J.J.

947. Lurch

948. Leif Erickson

949. Cousin Beau Maverick

950) In the series *The Fugitive,* David Janssen portrayed Dr. Richard Kimble. True or False?

951) In the series *The Six Million Dollar Man,* who was the character responsible for the creation of the superhero?

952) What type of airplane did Sky King use in the show *Sky King?*

953) What actor portrayed China Smith in the adventure series *China Smith?*

954) What actress did the commercials for 20 Mule Team Borax during the western *Death Valley Days?*

955) What actor portrayed Agent 86 in the sitcom *Get Smart?*

956) What was the name of the U.S. Government spy agency in the intrigue series *It Takes a Thief?*
    a. SIA
    b. AIS
    c. ISA
    d. none of these

957) What character did Denver Pyle portray in the western *The Life and Legend of Wyatt Earp?*

958) Who played Laura Petrie in the sitcom *The Dick Van Dyke Show?*

959) The Anderson's two older children decided to board at a distant college in the sitcom *Father Knows Best.* True or False?

960) Who portrayed Ellie Barnes in the sitcom *The Joey Bishop Show?*

961) What was the name of the schooner in the series *Adventures in Paradise?*

. . . Answers

950. True

951. Dr. Rudy Wells

952. Cessna

953. Dan Duryea

954. Rosemary DeCamp

955. Don Adams

956. a. SIA

957. Ben Thompson

958. Mary Tyler Moore

959. False, they elected to go to their town's own state college

960. Abby Dalton

961. *Tiki*

962) What famous TV entertainer was known for the slight tap of his hand to his cheek as a comedic gesture?

963) Who was the actor who played Lt. Columbo in the series *Columbo?*

964) Buddy Hackett, Paul Lynde and Carol Burnett played characters in this sitcom of the late 1950's which was based in a hotel of New York.

965) In the *Here's Lucy* show, what actress and actor portrayed Kim Carter and Craig Carter?

966) In the early days of television, who was known as "Mr. Television"?

967) Who played the original Captain Video in the childrens' series *Captain Video and His Video Rangers?*

968) What was the nickname of Francis Marion on the *Walt Disney* adventure shows?

969) Professor Kingsfield was an authority on criminal law in the series *The Paper Chase*. True or False?

970) Who portrayed Dr. Sellers in the drama *Dr. Simon Locke?*

971) What was the name of the Munsters' son in the sitcom *The Munsters?*

972) Who were the three N.Y.P.D. detectives in the police series *N.Y.P.D.?*

... *Answers*

962. Jack Benny

963. Peter Falk

964. *Stanley*

965. Kim (Lucie Arnaz) and Craig (Desi Arnaz, Jr.)

966. Milton Berle, *The Milton Berle Show*

967. Richard Coogan

968. "Swamp Fox"

969. False, contract law

970. Jack Albertson

971. Edward Wolfgang (Eddie) Munster

972. Mike Haines, Jeff Ward, Johnny Corso

973) Of the three different dogs that filled the role of Rin Tin Tin in *The Adventures of Rin Tin Tin,* how many were descendants of the original dog?

    a. one
    b. two
    c. three
    d. none

974) What was the name of the quiz show whose theme song was "Thinking of You" and was emceed by Kay Kyser and Tennessee Ernie Ford?

975) "Bubbles in the Champagne" was the theme song in *The Lawrence Welk Show.* True or False?

976) What actor portrayed Bronco Layne in the western *Bronco?*

977) Ann Marie and Don Hollinger were characters in this series about a young woman who left her home in the suburbs to start a career in New York City.

978) Who was Irma's first roommate in the sitcom *My Friend Irma?*

979) What was the name of the captain in the science fiction series *Land of the Giants?*

    a. Steve Burton
    b. Mark Wilson
    c. Barry Lockridge
    d. Dan Erikson

980) Lisa Lu replaced Kam Tong in the western *Have Gun Will Travel.* What was her name which was slightly different from her male predecessor's?

... *Answers*

973. b. two

974. *Kay Kyser's Kollege of Musical Knowledge*

975. False, "Bubbles in the Wine"

976. Ty Hardin

977. *That Girl*

978. Jane Stacy

979. a. Steve Burton

980. Hey Girl

981) How many millions did the Clampetts receive for their oil rich land in *The Beverly Hillbillies?*
    a. $10,000,000
    b. $15,000,000
    c. $20,000,000
    d. $25,000,000

982) Where was Dagwood employed in the sitcom *Blondie?*

983) Who portrayed Andy Thompson in the series *The Headmaster?*

984) What company was the major sponsor for the show *Studio One?*

985) What actor portrayed Tonto in the western *The Lone Ranger?*

986) In this quiz show hosted by Jack Barry, a joker on the machine could double or triple the pot.

987) In the series *Topper*, what was the name of the St. Bernard dog?

988) In the sitcom *My Favorite Martian*, Mrs. Lorelei Brown was portrayed by this actress who also played Blondie in the sitcom *Blondie?*

989) Who played Eddie's friend, Joey Kelly, in the series *The Courtship of Eddie's Father?*

990) What is the name of the medical show which became the first ABC series ever to reach a number one position above all other TV programs for a full season (1970-1971)?

991) What superagent did David McCallum portray in the spy series *The Man from U.N.C.L.E.?*

. . . Answers

981. d. $25,000,000

982. Dithers Construction Co.

983. Andy Griffith

984. Westinghouse

985. Jay Silverheels

986. *The Joker's Wild*

987. Neil

988. Pamela Britton

989. Jodie Foster

990. *Marcus Welby, M.D.*

991. Illya Kuryakin

992) Who was the president from which James T. West and Artemus Gordon received assignments in the western *The Wild Wild West?*

993) What was the name of the orphaned boy adopted by the Rubbles in the cartoon series *The Flintstones?*

994) What was Millie's job in the sitcom *Meet Millie?*
   a. housekeeper
   b. barmaid
   c. waitress
   d. secretary

995) Tony Nelson and Jeannie were married in the sitcom *I Dream of Jeannie.* True or False?

996) What was the name of Clarence Day's wife in the sitcom *Life With Father?*

997) What actor portrayed Alexander McKeag in the drama *Centennial?*

998) What were the names of the Goldbergs' two children in the sitcom *The Goldbergs?*

999) Sue Randall portrayed this schoolteacher of Beaver's in the sitcom *Leave It to Beaver.*

1000) What was the name of the company that Joe Gerard owned in the sitcom *Rhoda?*

1001) What was the longest continuously running police show in TV history?

. . . Answers

992. President Grant

993. Bamm Bamm

994. d. secretary

995. True

996. Vinnie

997. Richard Chamberlain

998. Sammy and Rosalie

999. Miss Landers

1000. New York Wrecking Company

1001. *Hawaii Five-O*

1002) What role did Phyllis Lindstrom play in the sitcom *The Mary Tyler Moore Show?*
    a. newswriter
    b. anchorwoman
    c. landlady
    d. maid

1003) What was the name of the dog on *The Roy Rogers Show?*

1004) Tony Forsythe plays Bentley Gregg in *Bachelor Father.* True or False?

1005) What type of business did Mindy's father own in the sitcom *Mork & Mindy?*
    a. grocery store
    b. hobby shop
    c. bedding shop
    d. music store

1006) What was the name of Dick West's horse in the series *The Range Rider?*

1007) What was the name of Nancy's brother in the drama *Family?*

1008) The following three titles are indicative of the type of playlets presented in this comedy series which was first telecast in 1969: "Love and a Couple of Couples, Love and the Hustler, and Love and the Pill."

1009) Audra Barkley was played by which actress in the western *The Big Valley?*

1010) What actor portrayed Sgt. Joe Friday in the police drama *Dragnet?*

. . . *Answers*

1002. c. landlady

1003. Bullet

1004. False, John Forsythe

1005. d. music store

1006. Lucky

1007. Willie

1008. *Love, American Style*

1009. Linda Evans

1010. Jack Webb

QUESTIONS

1011) What was Joe in *The Jackie Gleason Show?*
  a. repairman
  b. truck driver
  c. chef
  d. none of these

1012) What actor portrayed Kwai Chang Caine in the series *Kung Fu?*

1013) Who was the host and narrator of the documentary series *In Search of . . .?*

1014) Mrs. MacDonald was the Lane's housekeeper in the *Patty Duke Show* and was portrayed by this actress of Wicked Witch fame (*The Wizard of Oz*).

1015) *The Fred Waring Show* was always performed before a live studio audience. True or False?

1016) What was the name of the detective played by Joe Santos in the series *The Rockford Files?*

1017) What character did Eve Plumb portray in the sitcom *The Brady Bunch?*

1018) What was the name of the dog in the sitcom *The Governor & J.J.?*

1019) Gomez Addams of *The Addams Family* was played by what actor?

1020) Big John's second marriage was to this woman in the western *The High Chaparral.*

1021) What character did Arlene Golanka portray in the sitcom *Mayberry R.F.D.?*

. . . Answers

1011. d. none of these, he was a bartender

1012. David Carradine

1013. Leonard Nimoy

1014. Margaret Hamilton

1015. False

1016. Det. Dennis Becker

1017. Jan Brady

1018. Guv

1019. John Astin

1020. Victoria Montoya

1021. Millie Swanson

1022) What character did Michael Nouri portray in the drama *The Gangster Chronicles?*

1023) What was the name of Sky King's airplane in the series *Sky King?*

1024) What was the name of the restaurant located next to No. 77 Sunset Strip in the hit series *77 Sunset Strip?*

1025) Who portrayed Bob Landers in the sitcom *The Debbie Reynolds Show?*

1026) Maxwell Smart and Susan Hilton were later married in the sitcom *Get Smart.*

1027) What actor portrayed Al Mundy in the series *It Takes a Thief?*

1028) In what year did *The Adventures of Ozzie & Harriet* start on television?
    a. 1948
    b. 1952
    c. 1954
    d. 1957

1029) Who did Joey Barnes marry in the sitcom *The Joey Bishop Show?*

1030) Margaret Anderson was played by what actress in the sitcom *Father Knows Best.*

1031) Who played Christopher Colt in the western series *Colt .45?*

1032) Who played Dr. Leonard McCoy in the series *Star Trek?*

. . . *Answers*

1022. Charles "Lucky" Luciano

1023. *The Songbird*

1024. Dino's

1025. Tom Bosley

1026. True

1027. Robert Wagner

1028. b. 1952

1029. Ellie

1030. Jane Wyatt

1031. Wayde Preston

1032. DeForest Kelley

1033) In the sitcom M*A*S*H, Maj. Charles Emerson Winchester was from Philadelphia. True or False?

1034) Who was *not* a moderator in the quiz show *I've Got a Secret?*
   a. Garry Moore
   b. John Daly
   c. Steve Allen
   d. Bill Cullen

1035) What actor portrayed John Novak in the series *Mr. Novak?*

1036) To what city and precinct was Car 54 assigned in the sitcom *Car 54, Where Are You?*

1037) Name the character and actor who was the original wagonmaster in the western *Wagon Train.*

1038) Who were the two truck drivers in the series *Movin' On?*

1039) This female character was an editorial assistant in the series *The Name of the Game.*

1040) In *The Adventures of Wild Bill Hickok,* who said: "That's Wild Bill Hickok, mister! The bravest, strongest, fightingest U.S. Marshal in the whole West!"?

1041) What was the name of the orphan in the comedy series *Kentucky Jones?*

1042) The cases in the police series *The Lawless Years* were based on the exploits of this real-life New York cop.

1043) In the sitcom *Bringing Up Buddy,* what were the names of the two maiden aunts?

. . . Answers

1033. False, Boston

1034. b. John Daly

1035. James Franciscus

1036. New York's 53rd precinct

1037. Major Seth Adams played by Ward Bond

1038. Sonny Pruitt and Will Chandler

1039. Peggy Maxwell

1040. Jingles

1041. Dwight Eisenhower "Ike" Wong

1042. Barney Ruditsky

1043. Aunt Violet Flower and Aunt Iris Flower

1044) In the sitcom *That's My Boy*, Alice Jackson was a former athlete in which sport?
    a. golf
    b. tennis
    c. track
    d. dance

1045) Who played Grandpa Tarleton in the sitcom *Tammy?*

1046) *My Friend Flicka* was a story of a boy and his raccoon. True or False?

1047) What actor portrayed George Cooper in the sitcom *My Favorite Husband?*

1048) What were the character names of the three daughters on *Petticoat Junction?*

1049) At what fort was Sergeant Ernie T. Bilko stationed in *The Phil Silvers Show?*

1050) How many daughters did Larry have in the sitcom *Hello, Larry?*
    a. one
    b. two
    c. three
    d. four

1051) John Forsythe's daughters, Brooke and Page, were casted in the sitcom *The John Forsythe Show*. True or False?

1052) In the cartoon series *Jonny Quest* what was Roger "Race" Bannon?
    a. bodyguard
    b. scientist
    c. bulldog
    d. none of these

. . . *Answers*

1044. b. tennis

1045. Denver Pyle

1046. False, horse

1047. Barry Nelson

1048. Billie Jo, Betty Jo, and Bobbie Jo

1049. Fort Baxter, Kansas

1050. b. two

1051. True

1052. a. bodyguard

1053) What actor portrayed George Baxter in the sitcom *Hazel?*

1054) Dick Hollister of the sitcom *He & She* was a cartoonist who created this successful character.

1055) In the sitcom *The Tycoon* who was the chairman of the Thunder Corporation?

1056) What was the character name of Walter Brennan in the series *To Rome With Love?*

1057) *Noah's Ark* was the story of two veterinarians. True or False?

1058) Who was Joe's secretary in the police series *Mannix?*

1059) What was the name of the character played by Peter Lawford in the series *The Thin Man?*

1060) What was the name of the spaceship in the show *Tom Corbett, Space Cadet?*

1061) In what field did Julia make her career in the sitcom *Julia?*
    a. social work   c. psychiatry
    b. law   d. nursing

1062) What actor portrayed Thomas Remington Sloane III in the intrigue series *A Man Called Sloane?*

1063) Name the character portrayed by Mercedes McCambridge in the series *Wire Service*.

1064) Frank Lovejoy portrayed McGraw in the detective series *Meet McGraw*. True or False?

1065) This boyfriend of Millie's was also her boss's son in the sitcom *Meet Millie*.

. . . Answers

1053. Don DeFore

1054. "Jetman"

1055. Walter Andrews

1056. Grandpa Andy Pruitt

1057. True

1058. Peggy Fair

1059. Nick Charles

1060. *Polaris*

1061. d. nursing

1062. Robert Conrad

1063. Katherine Wells

1064. True

1065. Johnny Boone, Jr.

1066) Wayne Rogers portrays this character in the sitcom *House Calls*.

1067) What is the number of McHale's squadron in the sitcom *McHale's Navy?*
    a. 13   c. 17
    b. 15   d. 19

1068) Snarky Parker was a cartoon character in the series *Life With Snarky Parker.* True or False?

1069) Which actor in the sitcom *The Goldbergs* was accused of Communistic sympathies?

1070) What actor portrayed Jesse James in the western *The Legend of Jesse James?*

1071) In this discussion series moderated by Maggie McNellis, only one male was present to defend his sex and he was issued a toy horn as a means to signal his intent to refute the accusations of the women.

1072) What actor portrayed Howie in the sitcom *Mary Kay and Johnny?*

1073) In what year did the western *Gunsmoke* premiere?
    a. 1952   c. 1954
    b. 1953   d. 1955

1074) Who did Carl Reiner play in the comedy variety *Caesar's Hour?*

1075) In the police drama *Baretta,* who portrayed Det. Tony Baretta?

1076) At the conclusion of each episode of *Mork & Mindy,* Mork would say good-bye to his leader in this short, catchy phrase.

. . . *Answers*

1066. Dr. Charley Michaels

1067. d. Squadron 19

1068. False, Snarky Parker was a marionette

1069. Philip Loeb

1070. Christopher Jones

1071. *Leave It to the Girls*

1072. Howard Thomas

1073. d. 1955

1074. George Hansen

1075. Robert Blake

1076. "Na nu, na nu"

1077) What was the name of Barnaby Jones's daughter-in-law in the detective series *Barnaby Jones?*

1078) What actor portrayed Captain Amos Burke in the police drama *Burke's Law?*

1079) On which network station did *Rawhide* appear?

1080) In what profession was Bob Hartley in the sitcom *The Bob Newhart Show?*
   a. dentist
   b. psychologist
   c. teacher
   d. scientist

1081) What was the name given to the 16 beautiful girls in *The Jackie Gleason Show?*

1082) Who were Julie Willis's parents in the sitcom *Love on a Rooftop?*

1083) Kwai Chang Caine was born in China in the series *Kung Fu.* True or False?

1084) In the occult series *Kolchak: The Night Stalker,* what actor portrayed Carl Kolchak?

1085) What was the name of Flo's best friend in the sitcom *Flo?*

1086) In the *Foreign Intrigue* series who portrayed Robert Cannon?

1087) In the sitcom *The Governor & J.J.* what relation to Governor William Drinkwater was J.J. Drinkwater?
   a. wife
   b. daughter
   c. mother
   d. grandmother

1088) In the western *The Gene Autry Show* who was Gene Autry's sidekick?

. . . Answers

1077. Betty Jones

1078. Gene Barry

1079. CBS

1080. b. psychologist

1081. The Glea-Girls

1082. Phyllis and Fred Hammond

1083. True

1084. Darren McGavin

1085. Miriam

1086. Jerome Thor

1087. b. daughter

1088. Pat Buttram

QUESTIONS

1089) Who did Florida Evans marry in the sitcom *Good Times?*

1090) What was Gidget's full name in the sitcom *Gidget?*

1091) What was the name of the wrecked charter boat in the sitcom *Gilligan's Island?*

1092) In *The Jack Benny Show,* where was the vault hidden which contained Jack's money?
    a. attic   c. behind a picture
    b. under a rose bush   d. basement

1093) What instrument did Jack like to play in *The Jack Benny Show?*
    a. tuba   c. violin
    b. clarinet   d. piano

1094) "Plink, Plank, Plunk" was the theme song of this quiz show which aired for 15 years.

1095) This show was adapted from a book by Monte Barrett entitled *Tempered Blade.*

1096) Ricky Nelson's first name was Eric in the sitcom *The Adventures of Ozzie & Harriet.* True or False?

1097) Who portrayed Dick Starrett in the comedy *Dick and the Duchess?*

1098) What was the name of the character played by Rose Marie in the sitcom *The Dick Van Dyke Show?*

1099) Katy married the Congressman on one of the shows in the sitcom *The Farmer's Daughter.* True or False?

. . . Answers

1089. Carl Dixon

1090. Francine Lawrence

1091. *Minnow*

1092. d. basement

1093. c. violin

1094. *I've Got a Secret*

1095. *The Adventures of Jim Bowie*

1096. True

1097. Patrick O'Neal

1098. Sally Rogers

1099. True